Spirituality with
Clothes On

Spirituality with Clothes On

Examining What Makes Us Who We Are

Gareth Brandt

Foreword by
Marlene Kropf

WIPF & STOCK · Eugene, Oregon

SPIRITUALITY WITH CLOTHES ON
Examining What Makes Us Who We Are

Wipf and Stock
An Imprint of Wipf and Stock Publishers
199 W. 8th Ave., Suite 3
Eugene, OR 97401

www.wipfandstock.com

ISBN 13: 978-1-4982-0020-2

Manufactured in the U.S.A.   01/02/2015

To the women who have been most
significant in my spiritual formation:

my mother, who gave me birth

my spiritual mother Dorothy Schmidt Riemer

my colleague Janet Boldt

my daughter Sarina and daughter-in-law Breanne

and most deeply to Cynthia, the love of my life

Contents

Acknowledgments

SPIRITUAL FORMATION ALWAYS HAPPENS in community, and so also book formation. Thanks to all the people who have been part of bringing this book to print. The following people read and responded to chapter drafts: Janet Boldt, Angelika Dawson, Emmanuel Denguessi, Dan and Julie Friesen, Ashley Funk, Marijka Olson, Jennifer Pratt, Cornelius Teichroeb, and Leane Winger. Adriel Brandt contributed his copy editing skills and incredible grasp of the English language toward making my writing more readable. Thanks to Marlene Kropf for writing the foreword to the book and for modeling and encouraging contemplative spirituality among Mennonites. Thanks to the people at Wipf & Stock for their work and guidance: Matthew Wimer, Calvin Jaffarian, and Kristen Brack for a truly unique cover.

Although spiritual formation is a lifelong process and it would be impossible for me to name all those who have contributed to my life in a myriad of ways, there are some people who have indirectly contributed to the material in this book by contributing to my life. I would like to thank all the students who have been part of one of the many spiritual formation classes I have taught at Columbia Bible College over the past fifteen years. I have learned just as much from you as you have from me. Thanks to my teaching partners over those years: Janet Boldt, Erv Klassen, Karin Gregory, Carole Molcar, Stan Bahnman, and Kathleen Doll. You have not only been my colleagues, but my spiritual friendship group. In addition to the women listed in the dedication, a number of men have been mentors to me at key times in my formation: Leonard Plett at my baptism in Manitoba, the late John P. Loewen during my first ministry placement in Ontario, John Stoesz and Erwin Kroeker at Braeside in Winnipeg, Ray Friesen and Ray Landis during the brief but personally significant years in Saskatchewan and Alberta, and Ron Penner and Walter Unger who took a risk to hire me at Columbia Bible College. Numerous groups and congregations have also contributed to my spiritual formation over the years and I mention only those that are presently ongoing: Brandt and Penner families, The Party of Five, The Mission Springs Group, Emmanuel Mennonite Church in Abbotsford, British Columbia, and my colleagues at Columbia Bible College.

Foreword

WHAT HAPPENS WHEN CLOTHES wear out is that we cut them into small pieces of varying shapes and sizes and then arrange and stitch them into colorful, creative designs. Something new and unique comes into being—a patchwork quilt. The old is transformed. What would otherwise have been discarded finds new life and warms us for many seasons to come.

I often thought of patchwork quilts as I read Gareth Brandt's book, *Spirituality with Clothes On: Examining What Makes Us Who We Are*. Throughout the book, Brandt explores images of clothing as a metaphor for the diverse influences that form and shape our spirituality. Asserting that there is no such thing as "naked spirituality," Brandt examines the ways our faith is expressed by the costumes of gender, personality, family, church, culture, history, and contemporary philosophical movements. In the end, he imagines an integrated, mature spirituality in which we are clothed with Christ and Christly virtues (Colossians 3:12–14).

When I was a child, my younger sister and I shared a bedroom. Our bed was covered with a patchwork quilt hand-made by our grandmother. Before we fell asleep, we played a game: one of us would find a square of cloth on our side of the bed and challenge the other to locate a matching square on her side. Then the other was "It" and got to choose the square and issue the challenge. Night after night we explored the many colors and textures of our quilt, discovering the interrelatedness of fabrics and designs—it wasn't just a random collection of scraps and bits of old clothes after all.

Nor is our spirituality. Each of us is a unique, God-breathed creation. Even though we are part of larger family systems, churches, cultures, and nations, our faith grows in response to God's personal call to each of us. The Spirit of God woos each one as though we are the sole focus of God's attention. If I am a Spanish-speaking immigrant in a large Canadian city or an American whose ancestors crossed the Atlantic in the mid–1800s during the Irish potato famine, I will respond to God's love and call in ways unlike any of my peers.

Still, after acknowledging the uniqueness of each journey, it is useful to view the broad patterns that also shape who we are and how we respond to God. And here is the strength of Brandt's book: he does a masterful job of selecting salient categories of influence, clearly analyzing their potential impact and illustrating their effects with pertinent examples. He shows how differing approaches to Scripture create contrasting spiritual experiences in young people and adults; he traces how various worship preferences are linked to styles of personality; he examines the long-lasting spiritual effects of relational and behavioral patterns in families. And he demonstrates how our communion with God and others is skewed by living in consumerist, violence-prone North America. These well-reasoned chapters provide tools for interpreting contemporary experience, especially for understanding the complexity of faith development in a pluralistic, postmodern culture.

For those from the strands of the church where divine action is emphasized, sometimes to the neglect of human agency, Brandt's discussions of the role of personality and human development in faith formation may be particularly useful. Reflection suggestions at the end of each chapter offer opportunities for all readers to dig into the unexamined assumptions of our faith and world view.

In a patchwork quilt, every bit and scrap is essential to the beauty of the whole. Each square of fabric is unique. At the same time, the combination of distinct individual pieces is what makes the patchwork quilt a treasured possession. Each journey with God is one-of-a-kind. At the same time, each journey with God is also part of a larger creative unfolding of beauty and truth in the world. I commend Gareth Brandt's book as a wise resource for pastors, lay leaders, teachers, college and seminary students, and parents who embrace the mystery of such a paradox as they guide others to clothe themselves with a garment that will last: the love and compassion of Christ.

Marlene Kropf,

Professor Emerita of Spiritual Formation and Worship
Anabaptist Mennonite Biblical Seminary, Elkhart, Indiana
August 18, 2014

INTRODUCTION

We Are What We Wear

"NAKED I CAME FROM my mother's womb and naked I will depart."[1] In between, however, I am usually wearing clothes of some kind. What about nakedness of the soul? Is there such a thing as naked spirituality? There have been a number of books on spirituality published recently with "naked" in the title.[2] The idea of nakedness is not only attention grabbing in a sexualized culture, but nakedness symbolizes the values of vulnerability and authenticity—and a radical back-to-basics approach in a western culture that has made life very technological and complicated. "Naked" books attempt to get at the essence of spirituality that is at the core of our beings, often bemoaning the stuffy religious dogmas and tired rituals that we see on the outside.

Although this quest for nakedness is a good thing for our spirituality, I believe that there is really no such thing as a naked spirituality. It is impossible to strip off all the clothes of religion, family, culture, and history to reveal an idealistic pure connection with divinity underneath. Our spirituality is always shaped by the clothes of our experience. In fact, maybe by beginning to recognize and appreciate—even integrate—all the layers we are wearing we will be better equipped to find the authentic naked self underneath. We are what we wear: we cannot separate ourselves from our experiences and our surroundings. The quest of this book is to acknowledge that

---

1. Job 1:21.

2. Rohr, *The Naked Now*; Murray, *The Naked Anabaptist*; McLaren, *Naked Spirituality*; Boriase, *The Naked Christian*.

1

we do wear clothes; and, by examining them, we begin to understand ourselves and accept others who are wearing different outfits. In fact, as we mature and become aware of the clothes we wear, we become more naked; that is, more who we truly are! At the end of our journey—in death, in the presence of our Creator—we become truly ourselves. We depart as naked as we came.

We are all living in this in-between time where we are accumulating closets of clothing. Sometimes we wonder how certain outfits got in there, and sometimes we put on some brand new clothes that seem so "us." I am in that stage called mid-life where people begin to look back on all the clothes in the closet of the past. In that sense, I have been writing this book for most of my life. Even as far back as elementary school I can remember what I can only describe as spiritual feelings: a deep desire to connect with unseen realities beyond me and within me. I believe this is a universal aspect of being human, although I may have been more sensitive to these sorts of things than some others. My developing years included a rich variety of experiences. I grew up in a faith community dominated by a combination of evangelical revivalism and conservative Mennonite ethics that emphasized separation from the world. I rejected my upbringing with overtly rebellious activities for a few years only to be drawn back in late adolescence. My studies in developmental psychology and practical theology led me to a calling in congregational and denominational youth and young adult ministry, which I worked in for more than a decade.

Being one of the few youth pastors with a Master's degree, I was invited to teach a course on adolescent development at a Christian college. Research and preparation for the course helped to deepen and ground my youth ministry while also giving me a taste of what would become my path for the long term. I was especially intrigued with the application of James Fowler's faith development theory[3] in light of the other developmental theories I was teaching. This led me to focus on the intersection between spiritual formation and human development during my graduate studies a few years later.

3. See Fowler, *Stages of Faith*. This theory will be explored further in chapter 6.

My thesis was on the spirituality of young adulthood and highlighted the significant transition in faith that occurs alongside the transition from high school to college. Sometime later, I was invited to teach a summer seminary class called "Spiritual Formation of Youth and Young Adults" for a few years. The emerging language and awareness of a culture shift towards postmodernism in the 1990s added a cultural component to the course that was previously based primarily on developmental aspects.

This seminary course formed the basis for a new college course in the youth ministry department that I would come to direct. As a college professor I had the opportunity to explore other life experiences and factors that shape spirituality such as gender, personality, family systems, and the pervasiveness of consumerism. My own experience of healing from the trauma of childhood sexual abuse led me to a deeper understanding of how wounds can become part of spiritual formation. This book comes out of this senior-level undergraduate spiritual formation course that I have now been teaching for over a decade. While it is true that emerging adults are consumed with self-reflection, we are never finished, and so I hope this material is relevant for people at various stages and transitions of faith.

Even though I have, in some ways, been writing this book all my life, this book also highlights the greatest struggle—and maybe the biggest failure—of my life; that is, to be continually growing spiritually. How can I tell if I am growing or not? What does spiritual formation look like? These are questions we will explore. I embrace Lewis Rambo's observation in the preface to one of his books: "All scholarship is a result of one's own personal predicament."[4] Indeed, this whole project comes out of my own pilgrimage. It is autobiographical, as I believe all good art is, but I hope that in reading about my outfits worn through the years you will recognize a few familiar pieces of clothing that are part of your wardrobe as well.

We are born naked: we do not need to be wearing clothes to be a human being. Thus, our journey of reflection must begin with our

4. Rambo, *Understanding Religious Conversion*, xii.

naked selves. Some people may find this look in the soul mirror a little uncomfortable—in the first chapter I hope to convince you of why this look is important. A book uses words to communicate—in chapter 2 we will examine the kind of language we use to describe our spiritual lives, and how language itself shapes our experiences. The Bible has been a source for the spiritual formation of Christian believers for many centuries and so, in the third chapter, I develop the biblical picture of what spiritual formation looks like as a theological foundation for what we put on during our lives.

In chapters 4–11 will examine some of the items of clothing that give shape, color, and style to our spirituality: how do men and women relate to God differently; how does personality affect how we express our faith; what can we expect spiritually from people at various developmental stages; what are the unique contributions and expressions at each stage? For good or ill we are all profoundly influenced by our families of origin, regardless of how faith was taught, or caught, or ignored. Digging even further back, how have various historical movements influenced the way we express our faith? Today, we live in a time of significant cultural shift from modernism to postmodernism in the western world—how has this shaped our faith? We could argue that the most popular religion in North America today is consumerism—how has this influenced the way we live the Christian life? Finally, as we become more comfortable with the clothes we are wearing, we also need to examine those items that were torn—sometimes years ago—and stuffed into a drawer to be forgotten. How do wounds affect us and shape our spiritual lives? How can these clothes be patched and used for our growth?

The concluding chapter is about where we are headed: what does Christian maturity look like? It includes an exhortation from the book of Colossians to put on the clothes of Christ, as well as some suggested practices and rituals for implementation.

I invite you now into the dressing room of life. This is a very personal journey, so at the end of each chapter you will find some questions for reflection whereby you can look in the mirror without anyone else looking. Who are you becoming? Where is God leading you? Sometimes, the clothes we wear are laid out for us, but we can always choose how we wear what we have already been given. Sometimes we wear an outfit for a while and find out it just does not fit properly or we grow out of it. You are what you wear. Let us take a look at what we have on.

1

The Naked Self: Where Spiritual Formation Begins

THE QUEST OF THIS book is to recognize that we do wear clothes; we need to acknowledge all the things that shape our spirituality. As we examine these things, reflect on them, and sometimes even embrace them, we begin to truly become ourselves. While our clothes are part of who we are, we must begin with our naked self and nothing else. This entire process is one of self-reflection, but this looking into the mirror of our souls will not necessarily be a comfortable gaze. In fact, some of us—like I did in the past—operate with a theology that keeps us from looking at ourselves at all![1]

Why start with the self?

Spiritual formation begins with the self and ends in community for the glory of God. To be spiritually formed, we are formed into the likeness of Christ as the Christian Scriptures teach.[2] This is our goal in our individual Christian lives, but how does it begin? Any attendance of faith formation or nurturing of spirituality must begin with ourselves, though this seems so contrary to how I grew up.

---

1. This chapter is based on a co-lecture with my colleague Janet Boldt in an introductory Spiritual Formation class at Columbia Bible College, and my previous article: "Transformation: Becoming Who God Created Us to Be."

2. Romans 8:29; Colossians 3:10.

"JOY equals Jesus first, Others second, Yourself last." As a child, this formula sounded good. Other language used to talk and sing about the spiritual life confirmed this theology: "deny yourself; crucify the flesh; kill the old self; forget about yourself and concentrate on him." While some of these lines come out of the Bible, the emphasis was not always particularly biblical. This theology led to self-flagellation as an expression of piety and self-hatred masquerading as humility, and often paralyzed my spiritual growth rather than nurturing it.

On the other hand, our society tells us to do the opposite: "look out for number one; look after yourself first; I'm king of the world; I did it my way." The free market economy and the media bombard us with these messages on a daily basis. We live in a society that trumpets the rights of the individual. Western psychologists have told us that the highest good is self-actualization. Is this the only alternative, or can we find a path between self-deprecation and narcissism?

There is a universal quest to know who we are—"Who am I?" is one of the biggest questions of life. Our identity is at the core of our sense of well-being: it is how we make sense of our lives; and it influences our life goals, our perceptions of the world, and our relationships. We want to know ourselves and we want to become our true selves—who we believe we are meant to be and who God created us to be. There is a universal quest to be known, and we want others to know us too—evidenced by the millions of Facebook users, blogs, and millions of "tweets" sent out on Twitter to update people on the latest of what we're thinking or what's important to us.

We begin with self-knowledge because it is so closely related to the other big question in life: "Who is God?" The search to know God and to love God happens as we come to know ourselves, for we are made in God's image. Knowledge of God can awaken knowledge of the self; and the reverse is also true, knowledge of the self can awaken knowledge of God. "[The] discovery of our True Self is also at the same time, a discovery of God . . . Longing for God and longing for our True Self are the same longing."[3]

---

3. Rohr, *Immortal Diamond*, 13, 99.

In classical writings on spirituality over the centuries this has been called "double knowledge."[4] In spiritual theology, double knowledge refers to knowledge of God and knowledge of self. This longing to know oneself and God is reflected in the writings of the past. Augustine wrote in one of his earliest writings, "Grant Lord, that I may know myself and that I may know thee."[5] Thomas à Kempis wrote, "The humble understanding of yourself is a surer path to God than the deep inquiry into knowledge."[6]

The way we experience and express our faith is inextricably connected with our self-identity, and our self-identity is connected to who we believe God to be because we are made in God's image. Genesis 1:27 says that we are created in the image of God; thus, it follows that we get to know a small part of what God is like when we get to know ourselves. Each one of us reflects one small dimension of the personality of God. Since we are created in the image of God, to know God and to love God is to love ourselves: to accept ourselves the way God has made us to be. The greatest commandment is to love God.[7] The human quest is to know God; that is, to find ultimate meaning in life: a higher purpose for being.

The second part of the great commandment is to "love your neighbor as yourself."[8] We cannot love our neighbor as ourselves unless we love ourselves first! To get to know ourselves and accept ourselves, we must begin to discover who God has created us to be. This is a journey of self-discovery that takes some time. Though we are all different, it is not how different we are or exactly how God has made us that matters most; rather, it is what we do with what God has given us.

---

4. Reese, *Deep Mentoring*, 57–60.

5. Augustine in Schaff, *A Select Library*, 547.

6. à Kempis, *The Imitation of Christ*, 32–33.

7. Deuteronomy 6:5; Matthew 22:36–37.

8. Matthew 22:39.

The process of self-discovery

Most people go through a typical process of self-discovery that begins with a period of conformity or foreclosure. In other words, a person becomes a spitting image of their parents, or becomes exactly what their parents wish for them without any further exploration or reflection. Parents are a natural and unavoidable influence (as we will acknowledge in chapter 7), and it is natural for young children to idolize their parents (as we will see in chapter 6), but foreclosure during adolescence and beyond can lead to an unhealthy sense of self. Sometimes domineering parents attempt to force an identity on their children. A tragic example of this occurs in the movie, *The Dead Poet's Society*, where a teenage boy who sees himself as a poet and an actor is being forced to pursue the father's trajectory in business and engineering.

Individuation from parents is also a natural process. During adolescence this is sometimes expressed through rebellion, as it was for me. I became exactly the opposite of what my parents wanted for me, doing the very things they believed were the most sinful. I smoked, drank, and swore because they were overt displays of rebellion. I defaced church property by throwing hymn books around and carving in the pews because the church building represented authority. My band of rebellious friends and I made fun of those who were conforming by calling them "goody two shoes" and other less complimentary terms. We did not realize that our behavior was really at the same level—we may have been negatively attached to authority figures, but as closely attached nonetheless!

A healthier way of exploring identity is through a process of experimentation; a person tries out different personalities and roles in varying geographical and social contexts. This is very typical of adolescents who may be one person at home, another at school, and yet another at the church youth group without having any sense of guilt or hypocrisy. It is also possible to experiment with different personas over a period of time. I recall one young man who was part of our youth ministry through both junior and senior high years. He became different personas by growing his hair out and wearing scruffy clothes; cutting his hair and becoming a preppy with nice sweaters; then carrying a skateboard with the appropriate shoes, T-shirt, and pants below his buttocks. I remember one such transformation where he vocally announced his new persona at youth group. My dilemma of identity exploration during my youth was that my parents had opposite personalities and I was a combination of both. I preferred to be like my mother, who was extraverted, sociable, and articulate, and only in adulthood came to embrace the fact that I was actually more introverted like my father.

This process of experimentation can be aided by deliberate reflection on the journey of self-discovery. Reflection can involve experimentation with various roles, prayer, journaling, and times of silence and solitude as well as listening to mentors, family, and friends. Though this kind of reflection may be heightened during adolescence and young adulthood, it is a process that continues throughout life. For me, journaling has been central to the development of my identity. I began journaling on Sunday, July 13, 1975 at 11:28 PM and that night wrote out my autobiography, at least as much as I remembered, from the selective memory and self-interested perspective of a fourteen year old struggling with identity and self-acceptance. Here are my concluding lines that night: "Deep, deep down I hope I am saved sometime but right now I need someone, either Sharon, Julie, Lana, Irene, Corinne, or God. I am a dreamer and could tell many dreams. I have a dream far off somewhere to be something, but that is only a dream. You know, I really don't know what the hell I'm writing this for because no bloody person will ever read it anyway."

And as I have learned, it does not matter that no one else reads my journal; in fact, it is best that only God reads it. A journal is a personal place where I can truly be myself. It is a spiritual mirror for the things inside me that I can't begin to see, much less understand, unless I write it out in ink on paper.

The discovery of the self is not selfish

It may appear that this focus on the self is just pure selfishness—and it can be—but the discovery of our self is a winding journey, and sometimes a messy process. Bernard of Clairveax helpfully delineates this journey with his "Four Degrees of Love."[9] The first degree is rather selfish—to love the self for the sake of self. Love is a natural human affection, but to love oneself for one's own pleasure is indeed the sin of selfishness. It is then all about having our own needs met. Perhaps this is where babies are at, but we hopefully grow up.

The second degree in Bernard's model is loving God for the sake of the self. In this stage we acknowledge that all love comes from God and God is seen as the one that rescues us when we are in trouble, protects us, and meets our needs. We love God because God helps us. We begin to love God even if it is for selfish reasons.

The third degree makes a significant move—to love God for the sake of God. When God rescues us we begin to feel some affection towards God for God's sake. To get to this stage we begin to see how needy we are and do a lot of praying to be rescued, but we begin to love God freely: for God is good, not necessarily just good to me. We begin to develop a reciprocal relationship with God and are obedient to the commands of God. We love because we are loved.[10]

Bernard believes that the final degree—that we love self for the sake of God—happens rarely in this life, at least not to completion. In this stage we are of one mind with God in that we see ourselves the way God sees us; thus, we begin to take on the character of God. We lose ourselves and gain ourselves at the same time. As we grow in our love for God, we grow in love and acceptance of ourselves the way God has created us in love. This is not prideful or narcissistic; rather, it is true humility: seeing ourselves as God sees us in Christ.

---

9. A complete modern version can be found at http://www.ccel.org/ccel/bernard/loving_god.pdf.

10. 1 John 4:7–11.

To focus on ourselves does not mean we do so in isolation. We need each other. It is impossible to develop an individual identity alone. We need others to find out who we are: to compare ourselves, to hear from others, to interact, to learn from each other, and to be challenged by those who are different from us. The purposes of God are not realized primarily through individual spiritual growth; instead, they are realized through the in-breaking of God's reign into our communities and our world. Our personal formation is for the sake of God and others—which brings us back to where we started! As Parker Palmer has said, "Self-care is never a selfish act—it is simply good stewardship of the only gift I have, the gift I was put on earth to offer to others. Anytime we can listen to the true self and give it the care it requires, we do so not only for ourselves, but for the many others whose lives we touch."[11] Spiritual formation begins by focusing on ourselves and ends in joyful communion with God, others, and creation. The goal of spiritual formation is not self-fulfillment but harmonious relationship, and its end is the embrace of the other: God, our enemy, our family, our neighbor, and all of creation.

It is my theory that the nature of our personal spiritual lives has a lot of connection with the way we go about our relationships with others. We are not some pure objective machine that programmatically nurtures the faith of others—we too are fallen, sinful, degenerate, divine image bearers "stumbling towards ecstasy"[12] and consummation with God. We too are involved in the formation of our own faith. Our spirituality is who we are—we cannot extract ourselves from who we are when we relate to others. Our unique God-given personality, our gender, the culture and country where we are born and raised, our experiences through the life cycle (the joyful, painful and mundane), our primary relationships, the schools we attend, the places we work . . . all of these combine to shape who we are and how we live with others. The more self-aware we are, the more we can extend out of ourselves to help others.

11. Palmer, *Let your Life Speak*, 30–31.

12. This phrase is from Bruce Cockburn's song, "Wondering Where the Lions Are."

God has created us as unique individuals with unique personalities, but we are never finished products. There is a saying, "God
loves us so much he accepts us just the way we are but God loves us
too much to leave us that way." God has called us to change: not to
change into something we are not, but to become more and more
who we really are—who God created and called us to be.

The Greek word that is translated as "transform" in Romans
12:2 has also given us the word metamorphosis. Metamorphosis is
an apt illustration for spiritual formation. The caterpillar does not
even resemble its former self when it spreads its wings as a butterfly,
yet it is the same creature. It has become completely itself. So it is for
us when we are transformed by the Spirit of Christ: we truly become
our naked selves—who we were created to be. This is the process of
transformation that Paul is talking about in Romans 12:2.

I believe that there are too many people who have never
come to terms with who they are and are therefore unaware of
their unhealthy preoccupation with themselves in their relationships with God and others. Because they have not learned to love
themselves as image-bearers of God they are unable to genuinely
love their neighbor. By facing our own naked selves along with
our shadows, rolls and wrinkles, broken bones and blemishes; by
being honest with God and ourselves about who we are, we create
opportunities for authentic relationships of depth and health.
This is sometimes a very difficult thing to do, but until we do this,
we will (often unconsciously) continue to be too preoccupied with
ourselves. In other words, to get the focus off of ourselves and onto
others, we must begin by intentionally focusing on ourselves. This
is the purpose of this book—to begin with the naked self and to
examine all the clothes that we have put on in our becoming. Let
us get to know ourselves for the sake of God and others.

For Reflection

How does it feel to begin the spiritual formation journey by looking at yourself?

Do you agree that it is not selfish? Why or why not?

Who are you? How would you describe yourself? What do you like about yourself? What would you like to change?

2

Labels: The Language of
Spiritual Formation

I DON'T LIKE THOSE scratchy little tags that accompany the neck of every shirt I wear. Aside from the brand name however, there is some essential information on that label: the size, where it was made (for those who are conscientious consumers), what it was made of (for those who may have skin sensitivities or comfort preferences), and of course proper washing instructions that will help to keep it the same size and color over the years.

Although labels on clothing may be annoying, they are even more annoying in life. No one wants to be labelled. We do not like to be labelled because we feel like it puts us in a box or puts limits on who we are or will become. It is true that human beings are too complex to be reduced to a color, letter, word, or number—as some personality tests do—but we have to use some kind of symbols in order to communicate meaningfully about ourselves. Even a name is a label. We have to use labels of some kind. "It's only words, but words are all I have," sang the Bee Gees a few decades ago.

Words are labels. Words are one of the best ways we have to communicate. Pictures are good but they can often be interpreted in various ways. So can words, but with words at least we have some standardized meanings of what they signify. This book attempts to paint a picture with words of how human beings are formed spiritually. Words, as labels or symbols of a deeper reality, help us to understand and work with mystery. The label is not the shirt itself. You can rip off the label and it is still a shirt, but the label does help us identify and take care of the shirt. So too is it with words about ourselves and how we seek to make meaning of life.

Spiritual experience is something that is mysterious and hard to put into words; we need to acknowledge that all of our descriptions will fall short, but try we must. Augustine wisely said, "What does anyone say when they speak about you, my God? Yet woe to those who keep silent concerning you."[1] Words may be inadequate, but without words meaningless looms.

Poetry as the language of spiritual experience

What kinds of words are adequate for the task? This is not a book of poetry but the words will function as words function in poetry. According to Webster, poetry is "Writing that formulates a concentrated imaginative awareness of experience in language chosen and arranged to create a specific emotional response through meaning, sound, and rhythm." Spiritual formation is about the processes of the heart. Poetry is heart language. I love how Eugene Peterson describes it: "Poetry is language used with personal intensity. It is not, as so many suppose, decorative speech. Poets use words to drag us into the depths of reality itself. They do not do it by reporting on how life is, but by push-pulling us into the middle of it. Poetry grabs for the jugular. Poetry doesn't so much tell us something we never knew as bring into recognition what is latent, forgotten, overlooked, or suppressed."[2]

You may not gain any new information in reading this book. Nevertheless, I hope that you will recognize things you may have known all along, but were just not able to articulate before in quite the same way. In this sense it will give voice to your heart. The heart is rhythmic; poetry is rhythmic language. The particular approach to spiritual formation in this book will flow according to the rhythms

1. *Confessions of Augustine*, 45.
2. Peterson, *Answering God*, 11–12.

of the human life cycle in the context of family, community, culture, and history. In that sense, this book is written in poetic language. Why do I describe spiritual formation language as poetry? Poetry communicates experience not information, and our spiritual lives are primarily about what we experience, not what we know. Theology is infamous for its big words and lofty concepts; I prefer to describe spiritual theology, or spirituality, as poetic theology. Systematic theology is about God; spiritual theology is about the human experience of God. Most of the writing we read every day in the marketplace communicates information and data which we need in order to function. However, when we describe our relationship with God or another person, we need the language of experience. Our relationships are not about hard data, but about the poetry of experience.

Poetry begins with the impulse to relate to the other, to nature, to people, to God. Poetry uses metaphors; metaphors are about relating one thing to another, a direct comparison between unlike objects. Thinking metaphorically means making a comparison between two dissimilar things, one of which is better known than the other, and using the better known one as a way of speaking about the lesser known. For example, we could describe a relationship with God as "dry" or "fruitful." Clearly, a relationship cannot lack humidity or produce apples, but because a relationship with God is hard to describe, we use such common comparisons to help us out.

How else can we describe a spiritual experience or process but through metaphors? Richard Rohr answers by saying, "Metaphors open up the real thing we call God. Symbols bring things from the hidden unconscious to consciousness, where they can be operative."[3] Poetic language with its metaphors and symbols helps us to grasp the depth of spiritual experience. "Metaphor uses the language of sense experience to lead us into the world of the unseen: faith, guilt, mind, God. The visible and invisible, put asunder by sin, are joined by metaphor."[4] Language, especially language about God, can become idolatrous. This is why I am saying that this

3. Rohr, *Immortal Diamond,* 75.
4. Peterson, *Answering God,* 73.

language must function as poetic metaphor. "An idol starts with a mystery and fashions it into something that can be measured; a metaphor begins with something common and lets it expand into immeasurable glory."[5] We use words all the time to describe our experiences with God, and consequently, it is important that we recognize how we are using these words. They are not words used to restrict our experiences or someone else's—"this is how you are to experience God"—but to open them up to the mysteries of divine work in our lives. Keep this in mind as you read this book.

The shaping power of spiritual words

We have established that language is metaphorically descriptive of spirituality. Can the language we use actually shape us? How? I believe that articulating our experience of faith is in itself an important aspect of spiritual formation. This necessitates that we learn a spiritual language. Language is very important in coming to faith and growing in faith. In some ways language shapes experience just as much as experience determines the words we use to describe it. The words that parents, evangelists, pastors, and adults used to speak about faith when we were growing up have a profound influence on our spiritual experiences. For example, if you grew up with the language of "speaking in tongues" as a part of everyday experience, or at least every-Sunday experience, you are probably more likely to speak in tongues. If you grew up hearing talk of "accepting Jesus into your heart" it is quite likely that as a young child you knelt by your bed and "prayed the prayer" with your parents close by. Someone who had never heard the words, probably never had the experience. Language has the power to shape our experience. This does not negate the experience; it just helps us to realize the shaping potential of language.

To illustrate, let's examine a few key words that are used when talking about how human beings relate to God. The word "spirituality" has become popular and with that has often become

5. Ibid., 78.

very fuzzy and unclear in meaning since everyone seems to be free to define it as they desire. I am using the word "spirituality" interchangeably with the word "faith" and use both to refer to the human experience of the divine, or the human response to God's initiative. Spirituality is how I express my relationship with God. Here are a few definitions that incorporate some of the different dimensions of faith and spirituality. Each definition may not be as tight and clean as we would like but hopefully they give us a sense for what we mean when we talk about faith or spirituality. Helpful synonyms of faith are: allegiance, trust, loyalty, sincerity, fidelity, conviction. The anonymous author of the biblical book of Hebrews says that "faith is the assurance of things hoped for, the conviction of things not seen."[6] My graduate school advisor, Don Misener said that, "In contrast to religion which can be accepted or rejected, spirituality is like a belly-button, everyone has one." Kathleen Norris, in her very helpful book where she defines numerous Christian words, says that "Faith is best thought of as a verb, not a thing that you either have or you don't."[7] Simply, I see faith and spirituality as the human response to divine initiative.

Traditionally, spirituality has been primarily, and sometimes exclusively, about the human relationship with God. Initially, it is important to understand that biblically, it is rather a tri-polar spirituality: God, self, and community. Spiritual formation begins with the relationship with the self, is focused on the relationship with God, and ends in community. Our relationship with God is inwardly directed toward personal transformation, upwardly compliant in our experience of divine encounter, and outwardly committed to relationships of solidarity with neighbours.[8] All three of these are deeply intertwined and inextricably related to each other. We often cannot, except theoretically, separate them. They are inseparable and indivisible, although each of the three define and determine the authenticity of the other parts. "Tripolar spirituality

6. Hebrews 11:1.

7. Norris, *Amazing Grace*, 169.

8. This concept is best articulated in Augsburger, *Dissident Discipleship*, 7–22.

is the breakthrough in which: love of God transcends and trans-
forms love of self, love of God and love of neighbor become one,
love of neighbor and love of self become one, and submission to
God and solidarity with neighbor are indivisible."[9]

There are many other synonyms for faith and spirituality
which will be used throughout the book depending on the particular "clothing line" that I am examining. Here are a few examples
of words that have been used by practitioners in the field of spiritual formation. Each word choice reflects a bit of the theology or
strategy of the one stating it, thus we will be using different terms
to explain different things in the book.

The word "development" is borrowed from the discipline
of developmental psychology and seems to assume formation is
something that happens naturally or inevitably. Psychology and
spirituality are closely linked, in fact, psychology started out as a
branch of theology rather than as a science as it is now often seen.

"Discipleship" is a favorite word in the Anabaptist tradition
that seems to imply that formation is something that comes about
by learning from a teacher or mentor. Jesus instructed his followers
to "follow me"[10] and "learn of me."[11] Hans Denck's famous quote
illustrates the essence of discipleship: "No one can know Christ
without following him in daily life."[12] The word "disciple" itself is
translated from the Greek word for "student."

"Sanctification" is a long religious word with a deep history
in various traditions. Basically, it is about becoming pure and holy
through the intervention of God who does the work of formation.
It is sometimes seen as a process and other times as a "second experience," depending on the tradition.

"Conversion" is a popular word among evangelicals referring
to an essential and important, and often dramatic, initiatory experience that happens at a certain time and place. Apart from its historical baggage, the word simply refers to a spiritual change from

9. Ibid., 13.
10. Mark 8:34.
11. Matthew 11:29.
12. Fellman, *Selected Writings of Hans Denck*, 46.

one thing to another. The word itself does not prescribe whether it happens in a moment or over a long period of time. In his book on conversion, Gordon Smith points out that "most if not all people come to faith in Christ through a protracted series of events."[13]

I prefer to use the word "formation" to highlight the fact that spiritual change is a process that takes time, interaction between various factors (seen in the above words), and the creativity and energy of each one involved. In a sense all of the words above have part of the truth. Which words are used most predominantly will play a part in shaping spiritual experience. All of the words together give us a more complete picture of the dynamics of spirituality.

Case study of how language shaped my early spiritual formation

My early Christian experience was shaped by the language that was used by my church, my parents, and later by influential teachers, musicians, and authors. Having grown up in conservative evangelicalism, I was inundated by dramatic testimonies of conversion events that were lifted up as the norm of Christian initiatory experience, yet my own experience was that I grew into faith gradually through positive family influences and weekly Christian discipleship that was both modelled and taught. Unfortunately, I often felt inadequate in my Christian experience because I could not identify a dramatic or specific experience of conversion, and found it difficult to manufacture something genuine!

I grew up in a church that had revival meetings twice a year, usually just before seeding time in spring and right after harvest in the fall. These meetings were always accompanied with the obligatory altar calls where people would go to the front of the church with great emotion, usually with tears and sobs of remorse over sin and the desire to repent. We always knew that the critical moment was coming when we would sing,

13. Smith, *Beginning Well*, 31.

Just as I am without one plea,
but that Thy blood was shed for me,
And that thou bidst me come to Thee,
O Lamb of God, I come, I come.[14]

We did not sing this song at any other time; it was saved for the last night of revival meetings twice a year when the altar call was given. The song had at least five verses and we would sing them over repeatedly until enough people had finally made it up to the front. I do not remember ever doing this but I do remember feeling great emotion, sometimes even guilt for not going forward and wondering if I would suffer in hell forever as a result.

I read a number of spiritual biographies during my early adolescence about drug addicts and gang members in New York being converted. Oh what wonderful testimonies they had! I was fascinated by their stories of dramatic change from murderers to evangelists. Nicky Cruz's *Run Baby Run* was probably my favorite. He grew up on the mean streets of New York and became a gang leader with more than a dozen murders to his debit. His life was dramatically turned around when confronted by a charismatic preacher from Pennsylvania named David Wilkerson. Here I was—a plain Mennonite farm boy living such a boring life with no access to drugs or weapons or anything exciting to build a testimony.

I sometimes wonder whether my rebellious years were an unconscious attempt to create something from which to repent. During my adolescence I decided that the church and its faith was a sham. My personality was such that I felt spiritual forces keenly and so my rebellion was not a turn toward secularism or atheism but a selling out to the forces of darkness. I do not recall praying to Satan to help me do bad things but I was definitely in touch with spiritual realities, while at the same time making a big game out of the whole thing publicly as if it was all a farce.Smoking and swearing were the most overt forms of rebellion available to us in a rural community at the time, drinking alcohol was added when a few older friends were able to supply us with liquor, and reckless

14. Charlotte Elliot, *Invalid's Hymn Book*, 1836. See chapter 8 for a description of the historical evangelical revivalist movement which birthed this song.

driving was woven in when we got our drivers' licences. These activities continued for a few years until I had a personal conversion experience one hot August night, a Friday the thirteenth. That night included a lot of weeping over all the bad things I had done and recording my thoughts for posterity. I remember waking up thinking that the sun shone somehow brighter that morning, and that a huge weight had been lifted from my shoulders. I did not tell anyone of this solitary night-time experience until much later when I told my parents. After this I decided a more public display of my new commitment was needed. This happened when our youth group was traveling to a "Lundstrom Crusade" in a city half an hour from our community. I told one of my friends on the way in that I would be going forward at the altar call. I got a "Ya right!" of sarcastic disbelief in response. The band played contemporary music that included electric guitars, a synthesizer, and drums; it was pretty close to rock n roll! The last song was still "Just as I am," but going forward here seemed so much more interesting than in the midst of the voices of unaccompanied farmers.

The next day at youth group drama rehearsal, the youth leader shook my hand and said, "Welcome aboard." I belonged. I was in. I felt a deep sense of affirmation and passion for the new life that lay ahead. I did "fall away" numerous times in high school, getting drunk with my old friends, but always returning to the commitment I had made. On one occasion I even made a public apology in front of my school class saying that my behavior at the dance was not becoming of my faith. The school only contained a minority of "born again type Christians" and so there were some snickers even from the teacher, but I felt empowered by my witness.

My experience of conversion was clothed by a spiritually sensitive personality, the practices of my church, the values of my family, and the language and stories of the books I read. Was my experience of faith somehow invalid and inferior as a result? By no means! But as I learned "discipleship" language at Bible college, "development" language in a university psychology department, and "formation" language at a mainline seminary and a Roman

Catholic Retreat Centre, I began to see the larger context of spiritual formation. Learning different words helped me to become more open to new experiences and helped me to understand the experiences of the past in a new way. Language not only helps us to describe our spiritual experiences, it also forms, or at least influences, our experiences. We may as well be aware of these dynamics from the outset.

For Reflection

What language of faith did you grow up with? How has it shaped your spirituality today?

What other languages have you learned or encountered? How have they shaped you?

Which language do you wear with the most pride? Which language best describes your present experience?

3

Divine Threads: Developing a Biblical Theology of Spiritual Formation

THE BIBLE IS NOT a book but a library containing at least 66 books! There is, however, a story that that threads its way through the whole thing. Before we examine the variety of clothes we wear that make us who we are, we must consider this divine thread that has worked in human lives throughout history—and also in ours. The cliché that "God works in mysterious ways" is indeed true when it comes to our spiritual formation. Our experiences are like individual threads that God weaves together to make us who we are. "We are woven together in our mother's womb" and continue to be woven throughout our lives.[1]

In the Bible, we have countless stories about how others have been shaped and formed by God. While the Bible does not give us a formula for spiritual formation—though some days we might appreciate a simple twelve step plan—the Bible does give us some clues, and offers us fellow travelers to walk the way with us. What does the Bible say about spiritual formation?

Approaching the Bible

Many books have been written about biblical approaches to things, but we need to look at the Bible for ourselves. Any time we do a

1. Psalm 139:13.

topical Bible study we must be careful, because any time one is selective in choosing texts there is bias involved. In order to be representative, I have included an Old Testament narrative with male and female characters, a teaching parable of Jesus, a narrative from the Gospels, and a Pauline text. I believe that the theology we will glean from these texts will be consistent with the thread that runs through the rest of the Bible.

Before we begin, a few statements about how we use and interpret Scripture are in order. Firstly, Bible study is never finished—there is always more. "There can be no closure to the disclosure of meaning in God's written revelation; there can be no absolute knowledge within the techniques of biblical hermeneutics."[2] Secondly, the Bible must be approached with humility and openness: "The Bible is not an object for us to study but a partner with whom we may dialogue."[3] "Any systematic attempt to master the [biblical] text is not only violent but irredeemably impossible."[4] Thirdly, the primary purpose of Bible study is not to collect information or even to increase our understanding, but so that it might become part of our everyday lives. "The goal of biblical study is not theoretical knowledge but practical behavior"[5] This is also the goal in this chapter.

Read the following texts alone or in a group and consider what each one says about spiritual formation. Take note of any common threads. I have done this exercise in the classroom for a number of years and we have repeatedly noticed five themes. Each year we come up with new insights, and yet each year the main themes are consistent even if the language varies. Let me share those themes with you, referring to each of the texts as we go.

• Genesis 25:21–34; 27:13–33:20.

• Ruth 1–4.

• Luke 15:11–32.

2. Keith Putt, as quoted in Erikson, *Postmodernizing Faith*, 137.
3. Brueggemann, *The Bible Makes Sense*, 152.
4. Rollins, *How (Not) to Speak of God*, 13.
5. Kraus, *Using Scripture in a Global Age*, 52.

- John 3:1–8.

- Philippians 3:7–16.

Spiritual formation is a process

Spiritual formation is a journey: we are "pressing on toward"[6] our goal—union with Christ. Paul uses similar imagery in other texts.[7] Spiritual formation is more like a marathon than a sprint and it involves training, hard work over time, and stamina rather than speed. My best friend runs marathons and I remember clearly the first time I witnessed such an event. Despite not knowing all the people who were crossing the finish line, the whole spectacle was inspiring—it was all about finishing and cheering each other on. The marathon is so much like life: it is long and has a variety of terrain; it is run on streets through neighborhoods where people live and work; there are refreshment stations along the way; and each part of the marathon looks different and is run differently.

In the story of the two sons,[8] the prodigal runs his own twisted marathon. It seems he had to go to a foreign country physically to experience further growth spiritually. The process of spiritual formation may follow a crooked, unexpected process. In this case, there appears to be a single moment of decision, but the whole experience from leaving the security of home, setting out on his own, and experiencing alternatives and consequences, can all be seen as part of the journey home.

The stories of both Jacob and Ruth also involve geographical journeys. The forming of Jacob's faith is a long geographical and spiritual journey which includes: making deals with his brother, coping with the consequences, running away from his family, vivid dreams, marriage to two women, long hard work, economic success, independence, wrestling with God, and at last, a reconciliation with his brother. The story of Ruth begins with her

6. Philippians 3:12–16.

7. 1 Corinthians 9:24–27.

8. Luke 15:11–32.

geographical journey from Moab to Bethlehem, which symbolizes her spiritual journey and her commitment voiced in 1:16–17. She journeys from poverty and homelessness to home and fruitfulness—literally and spiritually.

A "new birth" is often seen as an instantaneous, pre-packaged experience, but it involves a long process nevertheless. Consider the analogy that Jesus uses of physical birth.[9] Birth involves nine months of waiting—with different trimesters and experiences, specific eating and exercising habits, long hours of labor, transition, the assistance of numerous others—and, finally, the birth, which ends up being quite messy. A new birth is a process: a wonderful analogy for spiritual formation.

Spiritual formation is God-initiated

In the parable of the sons, the father—who represents God—lets his son go, and gives the son his inheritance. The memory of his father is what draws the prodigal son home. The father is the one waiting, the one who runs out to embrace the son, and the one that initiates the welcome-home party. The father is the one who initiates at every point in the journey, though he always gives freedom and never forces his love.

The word *anothen*, used in John 3:3, is usually translated "born again;" however, it has a double meaning—also meaning "born from above." In the context, "born from above" is actually a better translation. Nicodemus misunderstands Jesus's use of the word *anothen*, interpreting it as "born again," which is why he wonders if he should "enter again into [his] mother's womb." Jesus corrects him by saying, "No, I mean born from above, by the Spirit of God." This is a common device used in the Gospel of John; as in chapter 4 when the woman misunderstands about water and in chapter 9 when the Pharisees misunderstand about light. Each time Jesus corrects them as he does here. This correct translation emphasizes that spiritual

9. John 3:1–8.

birth is the work of the Spirit—the Spirit labors with us in giving birth to ourselves. Spiritual formation is divine work. God is the initiator in the spiritual formation of Paul, Jacob, and Ruth. In Philippians 3:12 it is "Christ Jesus who [first] took hold of us," and consequently our "pressing on" and "straining toward" is a response to God's initiative. It is a "righteousness that is not [our] own" but from God through Christ's work on our behalf.[10] Jacob's journey begins with a miraculous birth.[11] Jacob tries to initiate the process of his formation with deception, but it only spells trouble: he seems unwilling to wait for God's action, so God gives him a dream and a promise.[12] Even the mysterious wrestling match is initiated by God.[13] The story of Ruth begins with divine action: "Yahweh had come to aid."[14] Yahweh is pictured as a nurturing mother hen with outstretched wings welcoming Ruth home.[15] God is the initiator in the process of spiritual formation in our lives also.

Spiritual formation involves human response

Though spiritual formation is initiated by Holy Spirit, human response is invited, even required, in the process. Paul uses strong language in Philippians 3:12–16, where he sees himself "pressing on . . . laying hold . . . wanting to attain . . . reaching forward . . . straining towards." These are all words of effort, hard work, struggle, and human activity. We are co-workers with God in the formation of our faith, we are not passive recipients.

Although it was the thought of his father's house that drew the prodigal home, he had to make a decision and make a move towards home for it to become an effective reality. It involved a turning toward home, toward God. In like manner we are invited

10. Philippians 3:9.
11. Genesis 25:21.
12. Genesis 28:10–22.
13. Genesis 32:24.
14. Ruth 1:6.
15. Ruth 2:12.

to say, "Yes" in order to allow God to transform us. As we see in John 3:9–16, human faith is called forth as a response to the birth of the Spirit. Faith and belief are verbs; they are actions. The narratives of Jacob and Ruth also involve their actions and responses. Although his responses are not always Godward at first, Jacob responds and obeys the requests from God. The wrestling at the river shows the great human struggle with divine things; in fact, Jacob is renamed "the struggler."[16] It is a good name for a person of faith and the "man" commends Jacob for fighting well. Ruth responds to the gracious aid of God with a solemn commitment to God and to her mother-in-law. She is the one who initiates going to gather grain for Naomi and the one who initiates the relationship with Boaz at the threshing floor.

Spiritual formation happens in the context of community

We cannot become spiritually formed alone. The entire biblical narrative is the story of God's people acting in community—sinning together and turning to God together. The early church began as entire households committing themselves to Jesus and holding meetings in their homes.[17] Both in the story of Ruth and that of Jacob, extended family is always present and part of the scene. Commitments to God are spoken as commitments to family. Alienation from family and God appear to be one and the same.

We see family imagery again in the story of the prodigal son. Even though the prodigal goes out on his own, he recalls his father's household while he is away and it draws him home to community and salvation. The son's return is celebrated in community with feasting and dancing.

Philippians 3:7–16 seems a very individualistic passage, but in verses 15–17 the nouns become plural: "all of us . . . let us . . . join with others." Even Paul's individual "Damascus Road" experience

16. Genesis 32:28. Israel literally means "one who struggles with God."

17. Acts 10:27; 12:12; 16:15, 31–34.

happened in the context of companionship, subsequently verified by believers in the city.

Although the new birth is often seen as an individualistic experience, it can also be seen as happening in community if we continue the birthing analogy. No birth happens in isolation: there are a variety of attendants, midwives, and family all in attendance. So too, the spiritual birth does not happen in isolation.

Spiritual formation is mysterious

We have developed a neat theological package about spiritual formation from our biblical texts. It is a process that is God-initiated, yet involves human response in the context of community. Nevertheless, after all is said and done, we still have to confess that there is a lot we do not understand, and spiritual formation remains mysterious.

I love the mystery surrounding Jesus's words to Nicodemus about the new birth. The birth from above is like the wind. The wind is mysterious—you cannot see it or predict its next move. The results can be seen, but how it happens cannot be explained. Unfortunately, we have trivialized "born again" to be a certain formulaic human experience, but you cannot box the wind! If you try, it becomes stale air. Sometimes, as in Nicodemus's case, too much of our spirituality becomes stale and stagnant with years of knowing all the right answers. The point of this story is that this birth is entirely different from what Nicodemus perceived, and perhaps also what we as the modern church perceive. The new birth metaphor for spiritual formation is a mysterious one that leaves room for many more metaphors in Scripture. Here are just a few examples: turning,[18] receiving a gift like a child,[19] selling all

18. Acts 2:38.
19. John 1:12; Mark 10:13–16.

you have and following Jesus,[20] drinking living water,[21] the blind seeing,[22] lost is found.[23]

Our other texts continue the theme of mystery—of surprise and the unexpected. In Philippians 3:7-16, profit is loss, and in death is resurrection. The Philippians text includes deep, incomprehensible mystical elements. How exactly do we "participate in the death and resurrection of Christ?" This is a mystery. In the parable, it is the younger, rebellious son who is rewarded instead of the obedient older one. The formation of faith does not always happen the way we expect, and maybe those who we write off are really examples of the faithful! Are we too much like the older brother and also have no room for the surprises of God's grace?

The story of Jacob includes all kinds of mysterious twists and turns that cannot be explained easily: dreams, changing spots, the wrestling with the mysterious man who comes from God. The story again illustrates the unexpected nature of the Gospel in that the younger son got the blessing over the older, contrary to the way family tradition dictated. Ruth is also an unlikely person of faith in the biblical context, for she is a foreigner and a woman. The book of Ruth is a very plain, earthy story, yet has deep eternal significance—she becomes the ancestor of King David and the Messiah. That is the mystery of faith formation: it happens in ordinary people but is mysteriously eternal.

Sometimes, as Christians, we have been guilty of forming the Christian life in our own image or in the image of a particular theological tradition. These texts teach us that, though there are certain biblical characteristics of faith, there is also great variety in how people experience the formation of faith in their lives.

The common threads that we have observed are that the life of faith is not an event, or even a series of required events, but it is a varied process, a journey with twists and turns. It is a process initiated by the Spirit of God and involves human response

20. Mark 10:17-22.
21. John 4.
22. John 9.
23. Luke 19:1-10.

to that divine initiative in the context of a supportive community. Throughout this entire process we are constantly aware of how mysterious and wonderful is the work of the Spirit.

For Reflection

What does the Bible mean to you? How do you approach the Bible? How has it been part of your spiritual formation?

What do you think of the five biblical principles of spiritual formation presented?

- Which one do you particularly connect with? Why?
- Which one do you have issues with? Why?
- What would you like to add?

4

Pink and Blue: Are Men and Women
Different Spiritually?

It all starts with those baby jumpers. How do we know whether to buy a pink jumper or a blue jumper when we don't know the sex of the expected newborn? So we opt for the more neutral yellow or pastel green. I remember when unisex clothing was a new and radical thing, but men's and women's clothing fashions continue to be, in general, very distinct—just think about what the celebrities wear to the Academy Awards. I decided to be radical at our wedding by having the men wear pink bow-ties and pink cummerbunds to go with the pink dresses of the bride's attendants. Though our culture has come to be more accepting of boys in pink shirts and girls in blue jeans, most clothing stores still have separate sections for men and women, and it's not just about body shape—it's also about style, design, and color. There are some basic differences between men and women; whether these differences are primarily shaped by society or by genetics—or even whether they should be discussed—will continue to be debated.[1]

1. One of the members of my reading group was opposed to the idea of making generalizations about gender in the first place, and wrote: "The idea of gender generalizations is obsolete in today's society. Women are no longer restricted to the house and are welcome to travel, build, and create; therefore, gender generalizations and stereotypes simply just perpetuate the oppressive restrictions of the past. Men are no longer limited to emotionless physicality; therefore, gender generalizations and stereotypes simply just continue a flawed perception of manhood that perpetuates misogyny and ignorance. I'm not saying my

In the rural community I grew up in women were mothers, gardeners, and homemakers, and if they desired to work outside the home they were nurses, teachers, cooks, or secretaries. A "real man" in my extended family was a farmer, carpenter, plumber, or a mechanic—some kind of trade that involved working with his hands: physical labor using brute strength. As a university student, I enjoyed my summers working as a farm laborer but was not invigorated by the possibility of being a farmer or a tradesman for life. My adventure was a journey inward. I spent countless hours during my teenage years reading spiritual biographies and journaling out in the woods behind our farm yard. I dreamed. I wrote poetry.

In general, boys want to grow up to be men according to the values of their surrounding culture. I did a few things during my youth to express my masculinity; for example, playing numerous sports with vigor, especially football, baseball and track—and I was pretty good at it. I loved the competition and the feeling of running full tilt in the open field. Because of my intuition and romantic nature I could also express my manliness through relationships with girls. While I had many girlfriends during my adolescence and young adulthood, too many of these ended as "just friends" because most girls probably wanted the jock as a boyfriend and not the guy who recited poetry.

In university I took psychology along with a class full of females—and I am sure the engineering department statistics were the other way around. I was invigorated by other students, mostly women, who knew how to articulate their feelings and get beyond surface things. The woman I met and eventually married appreciated my openness and sensitivity to her, while I was initially attracted to her because she knew how to throw a football! We

---

generation is completely free of those societal bonds, but why be part of their perpetuity? Filmmakers, writers, and creators all do this: "I know that females can be equally engaging, entertaining, and worthy of the role, but society seems to think that a man should be the main character, so I'll write one in." Applying gender generalizations accedes to the harmful continuation of the problem; it says, "I know these shouldn't apply, but I'll apply them anyway."

certainly do not fit all the stereotypes of gender roles.[2] So how are
men and women different?

How are women and men different?

How deep do the differences go? Are we different spiritually in how
we pray, worship, and express our relationship with God? I have
always been skeptical of gender differences in spirituality, believ-
ing that it had more to do with other factors such as personality.
This may be because I often did not fit the traditional stereotype
of a male with my emotive, reflective personality in addition to
my interest in poetry and the arts. I married a woman who will
happily do our accounting and look after our investments while I
cook dinner. However, through my work on men's spirituality in
my previous book[3], I am in the process of being convinced that
gender can also be a significant variable in our spirituality.

We must tread carefully in this examination. While there are
some obvious differences in our bodies—men have a penis and the
ability to grow a beard, women have breasts and a vagina—even in
this most obvious area, there are exceptions. Some babies are born
with parts of both genitalia that make it difficult to determine which
sex the baby is. Similarly, when we tread into other areas of physicality such as body mass—men being usually bigger and stronger,
women being usually more petite and lithe—there are even more

2. I have chosen to write about this very basic human difference: male and
female as differentiating sex and gender. I believe that Genesis 1:27—"God
created them male and female"—is symbolic of all human difference. Today
we have become much more aware of the fact that the binary categories of
male and female are often not adequate in describing human sexuality. People
who are gay, lesbian, transgendered, transsexual, bisexual, or questioning their
sexuality will be deeply impacted by these realities, not only for their sexuality
but also spirituality. There has been little work done to my knowledge on the
influence of sexual orientation on spirituality. I leave this for future exploration, knowing that for some readers the acknowledgement of male/female
differences in spirituality may already be a stretch while for others it may be
inadequate to explain anything significant about their spirituality.

3. Brandt, *Under Construction*.

exceptions to these generalities, and we have not yet even mentioned possible social, emotional and spiritual differences!

I have done some workshops on gender differences and spirituality. After stating the obvious physical differences I ask for random comments about how men and women are different socially and emotionally without trying to determine whether these differences are as a result of nature or nurture, genetic or cultural—this argument will go on forever because it is often very difficult to determine. The typical differences mentioned are that men seem more rational, logical, and task oriented while women seem more emotive and relational. Research on the Myers-Briggs Type Indicator indicates that all personality traits cut across gender lines—save one. When it comes to decision-making a majority of males tend to operate in the thinking mode ("T") and a majority of females tend to use the feeling mode ("F").[4] The differences are statistically valid but, of course, this does not mean that there are no exceptions, as other variables besides gender also influence any particular decision. If things are this messy in other areas of gender difference, can we even say anything meaningful about gender differences in spirituality?

Male and female spirituality

A few years ago at a faculty retreat, our dean had faculty members participate in an interesting exercise. She placed a number of random objects into a box, asked us to take one out, and, after a few minutes of quiet reflection, describe how that object symbolized our spirituality. It just so happened that my close female colleague and I chose the same object: a coffee mug. My description included a sense of emptiness and the need for filling. She described her mug as a symbol for hospitality and conversation. Is this mostly due to our different personalities or might our different genders also have something to do with it?

4. Myers, *Gifts Differing*, 66.

I participated in a spiritual pilgrimage with a group of adults from across North America some years ago. The majority of the pilgrims were involved in ministry of some kind, but the most notable demographic was that the women outnumbered the men seven to one. Why was this? The three of us men discussed this at the back of the bus—("Men have to be near the engine," one of them joked, even though none of us knew much about engines.) We agreed that generally women were more in touch with their spiritual center, and were thus were more likely to be interested in an experiential course on communal spirituality. We wondered whether one of the reasons men weren't interested was because an appropriate spirituality for men had never been articulated for us. This, of course, was my quest in the book on men's spirituality.[5]

For my last degree I did some research with young adult subjects. While my purpose was not to discover gender differences, it became a significant aside. I found that female students tended to be more interested in religion and spirituality than male students. Males tended to see their spirituality as an individual expression that was independently nurtured through personal practices, whereas females tended to see their faith as interdependent and were more open to being nurtured by others. Males preferred more traditional worship styles and historical language for God, while females were often frustrated by traditional language and were open to and appreciative of a wide range of symbols and creative aesthetics.[6]

Women's spirituality

Men and women express their spirituality differently. Most people would probably acknowledge that women are generally more spiritually attuned than men and more in touch with their inner self and their emotions. The feminist movement helped to bring energy and validity to a unique feminine spirituality. My colleague,

---

5. Brandt, *Under Construction*.
6. Brandt, *Young Adult Spirituality,* 57–59.

Janet Boldt, has articulated this unique women's spirituality in four simple points:[7]

1. Women more commonly express their faith through imagination and story, rather than abstract, analytical and propositional thinking. Since theology has been dominated by men over the past millennium, it has become highly systematized, making it difficult for women to express themselves spiritually.

2. Women more commonly use relational means of faith development rather than impersonal and abstract means. The coffee cup analogy mentioned previously is an illustration of this.

3. Women experience their spirituality as embedded in everyday life, as "ensouled bodies" and "embodied souls." It is ironic that women tend to be more in touch with their bodies as well as their souls, perhaps because they intuitively see the deep connection between the two.

4. A woman's faith journey is described as having unique movements. These are circular rather than linear and move from alienation to awakening to relationality and back around again.

She also articulates some unique spiritual challenges for women. In what has been, and still is largely a "man's world" (as unjust as that may be), women are challenged to maintain self-affirmation alongside right relation with God and others. Women also have to deal with the sense that their unique faith stories are often not validated, and at times even dismissed. Finally, women have the challenge of finding ways to live with integrity in the midst of seemingly impossible choices involving marriage, motherhood, career, church, and friendships.

7. Her sources include: Slee, *Women's Faith*; Conn, *Women's Spirituality*; Hess, *Caretakers of Our Common House.*

Men's spirituality

If women are claiming that there is a unique female spirituality then there must be its reciprocal: a unique male spirituality. What is it like? I am a man—my spirituality is not some separate compartment that allows me to be feminine in that area but be masculine in other areas. My spirituality is holistic: it is about who I am—all of who I am—not a specialized and separate compartment somewhere. Men—considered more rational, muscular, and task-oriented—have sometimes been considered unspiritual—with exceptions for priests, pastors, and missionaries. I do not prescribe to the traditional, machismo, head of the household, spiritual leader, bring home the bacon kind of men's spirituality, and I have questions about the warrior/lover/king/sage archetypes as the primary images of men's spirituality, so what is men's spirituality like?[8] Without simply reciting the mirror opposites of women's spirituality we need to develop our own short list.

1. Men tend to express their spirituality through tangible tasks rather than words and feelings. Too often, male interaction is on a surface level: we talk about sports in a bar after a few beers to relax us; we go hunting, or fishing, or golfing, where talking at all is bad etiquette. What is needed, however, is connection on a deeper emotional level. Men generally do not find it easy to sit around and talk for hours. Most men need something to do: a game to play, a project to work on, or a mountain to climb. Some of my best personal conversations with other men have been on hikes, work projects, playing or watching sports: when we are doing something together, when our bodies are engaged. It is easy for me to talk when I have a topic, a script, and a lectern or a pulpit, but when it comes to my personal life it is more difficult.

2. Men's spirituality prefers to build and construct rather than gather for conversation. My primary metaphor in writing about men's spirituality was inspired by my friends in the

8. Brandt, *Under Construction*. See chapter 2.

SPIRITUALITY WITH CLOTHES ON

construction industry. Some of the traditional male occupations—carpenter, farmer, ironworker—can become powerful and constructive spiritual metaphors, even for postmodern men in an electronic age.

3. Men see their spiritual lives as linear journeys with destinations and markers on the way. Men's spirituality tends to be directional rather than circular and relational. I need a spiritual—and sometimes physical—mountain to climb in order for my soul to come alive.

Men also have some unique spiritual challenges. We must get used to the fact that it is no longer a man's world where we dictate—we must see women as our different and equal partners in spirituality. With the rise of feminism, men began to articulate a unique men's spirituality in response[9], but the challenge for us is to articulate our spirituality on its own terms and not simply as reactionary. Perhaps the biggest spiritual challenge for men is to get in touch with their own pain. Men are wounded in many ways, but one of the most profound is described by Richard Rohr as the "father wound."[10] Donald Miller tells his own poignant story of growing up without a father and describes himself and his peers as the first fatherless generation.[11] Many boys are growing up without fathers or with fathers who are physically removed or emotionally distant. How will boys learn to be spiritual men without any positive role models? Men are wounded in other ways, and since we are traditionally known as the "stronger sex," our spirituality will be significantly shaped by how we deal with our pain and weakness.

It is interesting to compare two spiritual classics that have endured the test of time: *Pilgrim's Progress* by John Bunyan and Teresa of Avila's *Interior Castle*. Although they are at least a generation apart, each with specific historical contexts, and from different theological persuasions, it is still noteworthy that the male writer

9. The groundbreaking book in this regard was Bly's, *Iron John*.

10. Rohr, *From Wild Man to Wise Man*, chapter 12. See also Brandt, *Under Construction*, chapter 6.

11. Miller, *Father Fiction*.

uses the epic upward journey motif while the female writer explores the various interior rooms of a mansion. If these two ancient writings are used to represent a foreshadowing of gender specific spirituality we can see some significant differences. Although both home and journey motifs are valuable for both men and women, the journey metaphor is used primarily for male spirituality and the home metaphor for female spirituality. Different clothes are needed for the climb up a mountain than for decorating the rooms of a mansion. Gender will have an influence on how we uniquely express our relationship with God.

For Reflection

What are the most significant differences between men and women?

How might these differences extend to spirituality?

How do you identify with the male or female models of spirituality presented?

What could be added to this chapter to make it more relevant for you?

5

Wear Your Colors: Personality and Spirituality

I WEAR PRIMARILY BLACK jeans and black or dark shirts. I do like Johnny Cash, and when students notice my black clothing and ask about it I usually tell them to listen to his song, "Man in Black." He sings, "There's a reason for the things that I have on; I wear it for the poor and the beaten down." I am a bit of a dark personality: moody and introverted, identifying emotionally with those in pain—and I write this on a five day retreat of silence and solitude. Not everyone may wear their clothes so symbolically, but whatever one wears is symbolic to some extent. Our clothes do say something about us—we wear bright, formal, and festive clothing to a wedding; dark and somber tones to a funeral; and T-shirts with bands or slogans we approve of to a folk show. We all have favorite colors and designs that suit who we are.

We are all different personalities and we wear different clothes to match them. What is your reaction when you see someone with the same shirt as you? Do you want to get to know them? Or perhaps you would rather avoid them because you like to think of yourself as unique? You are unique, of course—there are no two personalities that are exactly alike. Having said this, however, there are some personality characteristics that are shared. For example, extraversion and introversion have become part of our common language and experience. Generally speaking, extraverts get their energy from being with people while introverts are energized by time alone. This is one of four poles in the Myers-Briggs Type Indicator that, when combined, give us 16 personality types.

There are many more informal personality tests using colors, animals, or descriptive words to help us to articulate our unique identity. I've always been intrigued by how different personalities live out their relationship with God. Although there are biblical principles and guidelines, there is room for a wide variety of ways to pray, worship, and serve God.

Since we are all made in the image of God, as we discover our human differences we also begin to appreciate the diversity and wonder of God. This is part of the double knowledge we talked about earlier. Genesis 1:27 says, "So God created human beings in the divine image, in the image of God they were created; male and female God created them." Human variety is part of the divine image. Gender is perhaps one of the most obvious human differences, but this verse could also say, "Extraverted and introverted God created them." When we get to know people better we begin to know their personality. We say that God gives us our unique personality, but God shapes it through the mysterious combination of parental genetics and the experiences we have throughout life—especially in our early years. There are large gene and experience pools—oceans, even—because sometimes children with the same parents are very different!

To get to know ourselves and accept ourselves, we must also begin to discover who we are, who God has created us to be. This journey of self-discovery includes learning to know our unique personality. While each personality is different, it is not how different we are or exactly how God has made us that matters most; it is what we do with what God has given us. How will we worship and serve God with our unique personality? The process of our faith formation and our spiritual expression will vary according to our personality. "Who we are is how we pray."[1] Hopefully it will also help us to understand and appreciate others whose faith forms differently and who express their faith differently. I believe that discovering some language to describe our unique personality

1. Keating, *Who We Are is How We Pray.*

and how that shapes how we relate to God is one of the most important aspects of the journey of self-discovery. It will help us to understand and appreciate ourselves and also those that we live and work with who are different from us.

The Enneagram

The Enneagram spiritual personality inventory does not tell you who you are—neither does it tell you who you should be, can be, or who God meant you to be. It is merely a tool to help in the process of self-discovery. "Ennea" simply means nine and "gram" is a picture, so "Enneagram" means picture with nine points. Thus, there are nine different spiritual personality types. I refer readers to the sources used for this chapter for additional deeper work with the Enneagram.[2] These sources will explain each of the types with more depth and also the relationships between the types as indicated by the arrows and lines.

The Enneagram is an ancient tool with origins in monastic mysticism as early as the fifth century, and for this reason there are many different versions and no exclusive copyrights or scientific tests proving its validity. It is not a uniquely Christian tool but it has been used extensively for Christian retreats and spiritual

2. Baron and Wagele, *The Enneagram Made Easy*; Bergin and Fitzgerald, *An Enneagram Guide*; Rohr, *The Enneagram*; Zuercher, *Enneagram Spirituality.*

direction, especially since its rediscovery in the twentieth century. It has also spawned various similar tools that use it as a basis without referring to it—tools using different language with relatively similar types or categories.[3]

I appreciate the Enneagram because of its deep history and proven worth over time, as well as its impact on my own life. The Enneagram is one of the few tools that not only focuses on the gifts and strengths of each type but it also reveals some of the unique struggles and sins of each type since it is based on the seven deadly sins, plus two. Our gifts and our sins are often two sides of the same coin. The Enneagram is not merely about self-identity; rather, "it is concerned with change and making a turnaround, with what religious traditions call conversion or repentance."[4]

We can simplify and introduce the nine types by first looking at three different centres—each centre incorporating three of the nine types. A simple way to describe each centre is by asking the following question: What would be your first response coming across a person in obvious distress, lying on the floor in a public place? Would you feel deep empathy and emotion for the person? Would you begin to observe vitals, mentally assessing the situation? Would you jump into immediate action by calling 911 or offering other assistance? The first, emotional, response is the "heart" centre (Types 2,3,4); the second, logical, response is the "head" centre (Types 5,6,7); and the third, instinctive, response is the "gut" centre (Types 8,9,1). This is a simplistic exercise but you can probably already tell that people giving each of the three responses might have different ways they relate to God, just as they respond differently to a situation of crisis.

Before reading the descriptions of each of the nine personality types below, do the exercise found in appendix 1 to help you discern your Enneagram type. Further quizzes and descriptions

3. Schwarz, *The 3 Colors of Your Spirituality*, lists nine different spiritual styles that describe how people most naturally connect with God. Thomas, *Sacred Pathways*, also describes nine ways to love and connect with God.

4. Rohr, *The Enneagram*, 4.

can be found for free on various websites.[5] It is important to spend some time in prayer and reflection with some of the descriptions as it is not merely a matter of completing a quiz and being done with it. Each description below traces the unique spiritual path of each type: how they relate to God, worship style preferences, and how they might talk about God. Each heading also includes a psalm for meditation that relates to that spiritual personality. The purpose of my order beginning with #2 and ending with #1 is to correspond to the three centres.

Those in the heart space (2,3,4) tend to appreciate a spirituality they can feel. They like to express their relationship with God through emotions, creativity, and relationships with others.

#2 "The Helper" (Psalm 113)

As the title suggests, Twos express their relationships with God through helping other people. They feel closest to God when they are listening to people in pain or engaging in meaningful conversation with others. They are encouragers with a unique gift for empathetic listening—the kind of people who are described as "always there for others." An ideal worship service for a helper is where there is an opportunity to minister to others through listening, prayer, or conversation. God is seen as a lover—one who listens and cares. The incarnation of God as a human being in Jesus, and seeing the Spirit as an advocate are very important.

The problem for Twos is that they can become so consumed with helping other people that they neglect to care for themselves—they deny themselves in order to please others. They fear being useless and as a result they may repress and ignore their own needs as they seek to find meaning in meeting the needs of others. The unique sin of the helper is a false pride that comes out in an

---

5. There are various free online tools to help you determine your Enneagram type: http://enneagramquiz.com/quiz.html
http://www.eclecticenergies.com/enneagram/
http://www.9types.com/rheti/index.php

exaggerated need to be validated. The spiritual formation challenge is for self-care.

#3 "The Achiever" (Psalm 128)

Threes express their relationship with God by doing things for God and for others. They feel closest to God when they are successful in accomplishing things through speaking engagements, acts of service, advocacy work, or whatever fits the gifts of the person. These are usually people who are ambitious in initiating relationships and activities for the sake of the church and God's kingdom. The ideal worship service for achievers would have a purpose and would accomplish something for larger purposes. Achievers will see a human need and get things done to meet it. God is seen as one who moves and acts in human history.

The unique struggle of Threes is a lack of contentment. The desire for getting ahead, accomplishing things, and earning recognition is so strong that they will do almost anything for it. They may be willing to become superficial or even practice deceit, usually unconsciously, in order to rise to the top. Sometimes they are so busy doing things for God that they forget to be with God. Achievers fear failure, so that they sometimes mask it with more and more activity and increasing levels of efficiency. The spiritual formation challenge is paying attention to their feelings and resting in God's unconditional love.

#4 "The Individualist" (Psalm 130)

Fours express their relationship with God through the authenticity of their feelings and their own unique creativity. They experience God through beauty, art, music, poetry, rich symbolism, or complete silence. They are people who will experience all emotions to the full intensity, particularly the negative and darker emotions. They have the capacity to lament with those who are suffering, "weep with those who weep," and also to appreciate the beautiful.

An ideal worship service for individualists includes space for each person to experience God in their own way, possibly through various creative means. God is worshiped as creator, and as one who entered creation and felt with us all the depths of human emotion. The dark side of Fours' spirituality is their darkness. They fear the boredom of ordinariness and so sometimes over-dramatize and intensify all emotions, which can become dangerous when those emotions are painful or sorrowful. Self-loathing can result when individualists spend too much time analyzing and reflecting on their own selves. Envy is the vice of Fours; they can become obsessed with comparing themselves to others. The spiritual formation challenge is to be balanced and to embrace the present and the ordinary.

Those in the head space (5,6,7) tend to appreciate a spirituality that is thoughtful, even if each of the three types is very different from the others. They like to express their relationship with God through ordered learning and logical articulation.

#5 "The Thinker" (Psalm 19:7–14)

Fives express their relationships with God by contemplating the eternal truths of God. They feel closest to God when they are reading spiritual classics, the Bible, or listening to articulate speakers. Thinkers have a keen sense of perception, not only from reading and gathering information but from watching people. They have a wealth of knowledge and wisdom to share with others. An ideal worship service for thinkers would include insightful readings, a well thought-out sermon, and ample time for reflection and contemplation. God is seen as all-knowing and all-wise, beyond all human comprehension, and worthy of contemplation.

The struggle for Fives is the tendency to be detached, closed to the input of other people, and reliant only on self-discovery. Thinkers can withdraw literally and figuratively into their own private world of thought, sometimes arrogantly thinking that others just do not have the deep thoughts about God that they are experiencing. Their root sin is avarice—not so much hoarding money or possessions as spiritual thoughts and ideas. The spiritual formation challenge for Fives is becoming open to the emotions and contributions of others, and sharing theirs with others.

#6 "The Loyalist" (Psalm 133)

While Sixes also appreciate thoughtfulness, they express their relationships with God primarily through commitment to a group or doctrine. They feel closest to God when they are participating in communal discussions, Bible studies, and rituals. Loyalists may be cautious about their loyalty, but when they commit themselves they will do so unswervingly. They make wonderful small group, committee, and church members because they are always on the look-out for threats to the well-being of the group as well as ways to make the group more cohesive. Sixes prefer worship that is familiar, structured, and doctrinally sound, where God is worshiped as the Holy Trinity: a community of Father, Son, and Holy Spirit.

Sixes are timid and suspicious of outsiders, and can become a hindrance to the growth of a group by being opposed to the welcoming of newcomers or those who are different. They long for order and certainty; consequently, they do not like to take risks or step out of the comfort zone of the group. Their root sin is fear or anxiety; therefore, they can be afraid of new ideas or new people. The spiritual formation challenge for Sixes is taking some risks of faith by entertaining new people or ideas.

#7 "The Enthusiast" (Psalm 98)

Sevens express their relationships with God through spontaneous outbursts of praise and thanksgiving. They feel closest to God when they are on some kind of adventure—promoting God's goodness and the joy of life. Enthusiasts have a tendency to focus on the sunny side of life and have knack for seeing silver linings in every cloud. They want to make the world and their community a better place and will multi-task with dizzying speed to achieve their goals. An ideal worship service for the enthusiast includes lots of praise music, words of exhortation, and multiple stimuli. God is worshiped as a great God worthy of praise—a God whose joy gives us strength.

Sevens do not like to focus on the dark side, for they fear pain and negativity and do everything to avoid these things. Their root sin is gluttony, with the tendency to live life in excess—never stopping to contemplate the aspects of life that may be unpleasant. Sevens can live in denial and may find it hard to sit still or to be silent, and thus become activity addicts. The spiritual formation challenge for enthusiasts is practicing discipline—especially the disciplines of silence, solitude, and Sabbath, which will help them come face to face with reality.

Those in the gut space (8,9,1) tend to appreciate a spirituality that is instinctive and active. They like to express their relationships with God by working for justice and truth.

#8 "The Leader" (Psalm 72:1–7)

Eights, as the title suggests, express their relationships with God by being in charge. They feel closest to God when they are aggressively confronting situations of untruth and injustice. Their passion for truth and justice leads them to stand up for the oppressed and downtrodden. Leaders have a strong sense of direction and purpose to their lives—they get things done. They prefer to live their spirituality in public and in front of other people. A meaningful worship service for leaders would be one where truth and justice are clearly proclaimed—ideally, led by themselves! God is seen as Lord of Lords and King of Kings, the Just Judge and Sovereign over the entire universe.

The legitimate use of power by Eights can become a lust for power where they will do anything to achieve their purposes. Leaders avoid weakness and helplessness and can become publicly insensitive and personally empty—void of everything that is not seen by others. The spiritual formation challenge for leaders is cultivating sensitivity to others and embracing personal emptiness.

#9 "The Peacemaker" (Psalm 131)

On the outside, Nines seem completely opposite of Eights, but on the inside they are very similar. They are both aggressive, but Nines are primarily passive-aggressive. They make excellent mediators because nonviolent resistance comes naturally to them. Peacemakers express their relationships with God by just being, and doing as little as possible. They like to see people in harmony with God, with each other, and with nature. The ideal worship service for Nines is a walk in the woods, a conversation with friends—anything that expresses solidarity with the other—or even a relaxed time of silence and union with God. God is seen as one who brings shalom, Jesus is seen as the prince of peace, and the Spirit is seen to bind us all together in perfect love.

Nines fear conflict and will avoid it or attempt to solve it at all costs—including the sacrifice of their own selves. Their root sin is lethargy and laziness. They can withdraw, become apathetic and reclusive, or beat themselves up instead of confronting the situation the way that a leader might. The spiritual formation challenge for a peacemaker is valuing their own feelings, getting up off the couch, and standing up for themselves.

#1 "The Reformer" (Psalm 125)

Ones express their relationship with God by living carefully and uprightly—they are often known as perfectionists. They feel closest to God when their lives are orderly and they are practicing justice. They have strong moral standards for themselves and for others. Reformers are very sensitive to biblical principles and commands and are careful to obey them. They are always looking for ways to improve themselves, and their ideal worship service includes tangible guidance for how to live better or how to bring justice to the world. God is seen as holy, righteous, and passionate for justice.

The problem for Ones is that they never achieve the moral perfection they hold so dear and are therefore never quite satisfied. Anger is the root sin of Ones and they can become resentful and bitter towards others and loathing of themselves for not meeting up to God's—and their own—high standards. The spiritual formation challenge for reformers is accepting themselves the way God has made them and simply loving themselves as they are with all their defects and foibles.

Case Study of a Four

It was difficult for me, a "Flaming Four," to describe each of the nine types objectively and emotionlessly. Fours are those who are expressive and passionate, who like to be known as unique—they are called individualists for a reason! Now you know the mystery of why I wear the kind of clothing I described in the opening lines. When I first encountered the Enneagram almost twenty years ago, it not only helped me to understand and appreciate myself, it helped me to negotiate my way through a difficult pre-midlife crisis. I began to understand that this personality was strongly shaped through my early experience of childhood trauma. As I grew stronger, I was empowered to be able to recognize and deal with the root sin of this type; that is, comparing myself to others and envying those who do things better. Through experiencing a dark time in my life I was led to face the dark side of my spiritual personality: my propensity towards anxiety and depression. Yet it is not darkness and melancholia that my personality fears the most—it is ordinariness. I want everything to be dramatic, and sometimes my moods swing from pole to pole as a result. The spiritual formation challenge for my life is to embrace the ordinary—seeing the beauty and profundity in the mundane events of daily life. I'm writing this in the midst of my sabbatical, when I'm getting cabin fever because two speaking engagements were cancelled due to weather and I am not even able to focus on creative writing as much as I would like because I have a sick child to care for! My present Lent practice and my challenge to embrace the ordinary are calling me to be content with this, and to be open to God's work in my life through these less-than-spectacular circumstances.

We all wear different personal clothing. Each spiritual personality relates to God in their own unique way and prefers certain ways of worshiping and connecting with God and others. Each spiritual personality also struggles with unique sins and tendencies that might draw one away from God. Sometimes the best way we grow is to engage in a practice that is not a natural fit for us, as I described doing for myself. These different personality types will hopefully affirm the others for their unique gifts and connections while also challenging the others to grow in ways that stretch us all and deepen us to become more whole and human.

For Reflection

Which of the nine types do you identify with most closely? How do you feel about being this type?

When do you feel closest to God? What are your unique struggles?

How will you respond to your unique spiritual formation challenges?

6

Seasonal Attire: The Spirituality
of Life's Stages

I GREW UP ON the Canadian prairies, where there are four very distinct seasons. In the winter that lasts from November to April, it is bitterly cold. Spring is usually quick and messy: melting snow leaving mud and soft roads for those in the country and salt, sand, garbage, and potholes for those who live in the city. The summers are full of glorious sweltering hot days; evenings dominated by mosquitos; with nights that are generally cool, but muggy when a thunder storm is coming. The autumn is crisp and cool as children head back to school.

We had distinct clothing that went with each season. In winter we had parkas, scarves, toques, mittens, thick socks, long sleeved sweaters, boots, even special one-piece underwear that covered the entire body. This clothing was packed away during the spring and summer because it was only needed for half of the year. In spring, out came the rubber boots, rain jackets, splash pants, and short sleeved shirts. We could shed some clothing during the summer as we went barefoot and wore short pants and short-sleeved, light weight cotton shirts. In fall, some of the winter wear would come out, although we were never quite sure what to wear because of the fickleness of prairie snow: it could come in October or we could get a warm spell in late November when all the snow would melt. Every season had its specialized clothing for the temperature and the elements.

I don't know who it was who first articulated the idea that human life also has its seasons, but since the advent of developmental psychology just over one hundred years ago we have become more conscious of the stages or seasons of life. Daniel Levinson did a longitudinal study and presented this idea in his book and many others have followed.[1] My favorite subjects in university were the developmental psychology courses, and I took all of them—childhood, adolescence, adulthood, and aging. It was fascinating! I was intrigued by the theories of Piaget and cognitive development, Erik Erikson's psycho-social development, and Kohlberg's theory of moral development. One of my professors even presented a brand new theory based on these structural developmental theorists—James Fowler's theory of faith development. I was hooked!

James Fowler describes himself as a theologian first and a psychologist second and his theory has been widely critiqued and utilized by educators, pastors, counsellors, and scholars from various fields. Since discovering Fowler, I have encountered many other developmental stage approaches to spiritual formation. While they are necessarily general, they offer many insights into how people express their spirituality in different seasons of life. They have helped me both to understand myself and to minister to people in age appropriate ways. I believe that my sensitivity to where youth were at in their spiritual development was better training for my career in youth ministry than all the "tricks of the trade" courses I could have taken.

Fowler's theory of faith development

I will be using James Fowler's stages of faith as my primary grid to look at seasonal spirituality, using my own descriptions and augmenting it with some material from other theories that make some unique contributions.[2] A few definitions and disclaimers are necessary before we begin the stages.

1. Levinson, *The Seasons of a Man's Life.*
2. The following books have all contributed to my understanding: Balswick, et al. *The Reciprocating Self;* Ford, *Life Spirals;* Hughes, *God of Surprises,*

Fowler, as all structural theorists do, claims universal relevance and application of his theory. In order to do this, he distinguishes between religion, belief, and faith. Religion is the form of faith: the cumulative traditions of a faith group that includes scriptures, laws, myths, music, rituals, rites, creeds, architecture, etc. Belief is the content of faith: the holding of certain ideas and the translation of faith into concepts and propositions; as in, a statement of faith or a confession of faith.

Faith itself is deeper and more personal than religion and belief. Although they are reciprocal and dynamic, each grows or renews through its interaction with the other. Faith is a quality of the person—a worldview, the patterned process by which we find life meaningful. "Faith is the most fundamental category in the human quest for relation to transcendence. Faith, it appears, is generic, a universal feature of human living, recognizably similar everywhere despite the remarkable variety of forms and contents of religion and belief."[3]

We are persons of faith before we are Christian, or Jew, or Muslim, or even atheist. According to Fowler's definition, all people have faith because all people live for something—even if it is only themselves or simple survival. Some questions Fowler uses to get in touch with a person's faith: What are you spending and being spent for? What gets your best time and energy? What causes, dreams, goals or institutions are you pouring out your life for? What power or powers do you fear or dread? Which ones do you rely on and trust? To what or who are you committed to in life, in death? What is your purpose in life?

Of course, any theory that is worth anything will be critiqued, and there are many critiques of Fowler's theory. First of all, his definition of faith does not seem to be a distinct category, but seems to include everything from cognitive to social and moral; seeming, therefore, to be a human activity rather than a gift of God. Additionally, it is very difficult, if not impossible, to separate the structure

10–25; Hagberg and Guelich, *The Critical Journey*; Stephen Jones, *Faith Shaping*; Parks, *Big Questions*.

3. Fowler, *Stages of Faith*, 14.

of faith from its content and form. Fowler's definition of generic faith—although not one I would wholly embrace as adequate from a Christian perspective—is necessary for the validity of his theory. For that purpose we can accept it, acknowledging that we may want to work with a deeper definition that includes the affective dimension as well as the dimensions of religion and belief.

Fowler's theory has also been critiqued by feminists and those from non-western cultures as being too individualistic and hierarchical. It focuses on cognitive, intellectual knowing, and not enough on affective or relational elements. Healthy connectedness is just as much a sign of faith maturity as individuation.[4] Any time we have a stage theory it always seems like the next one is better than the last one—although he does not say that—and so there is a danger of ageism. It is also important to note that spiritual formation isn't just about moving through stages but about developing character. And what about sin? Growth is much messier than simply development.

Despite the critiques, I believe that Fowler's theory has a lot to offer to us in our understanding of how faith forms in western cultures. It is a risky and revolutionary theory in many ways, and since it is, in some ways, a first, it can always be improved on—Fowler himself has listened to critiques and has reworked and added to his theory. I believe it can have a profound effect on our self-understanding and ministry with people. It is also important to remember that there is always some distance between the models and the realities they represent, but a model does help us work with a mystery.

Winter

Undifferentiated Faith (infancy)

Fowler calls this a pre stage because it is very difficult to do any empirical research on faith with subjects who have not yet developed language or other forms of symbolic communication. I

---

4. This is the main thesis in Balswick, et al., *The Reciprocating Self.* See chapter 2.

call it winter because faith lays dormant, waiting to be formed. Faith is undifferentiated because an infant is completely dependent on the mother and other caregivers for everything: there is complete mutuality and trust. This does not mean that this early stage is irrelevant to faith development. Just as prenatal activities can impact the baby in the womb, the consistent and trustworthy care given to a newborn lays the groundwork for later faith development. The gift that infants contribute to the world is the sense of purity, innocence, and complete dependence that they exhibit. This is a quality that is easily lost as we grow older, though it can continue to be cultivated.

Spring

1. Intuitive-Projective Faith (early childhood)

Faith springs to life with self-awareness and the beginning of speech and communication. This stage usually begins around age two until the first few years of formal education, although the effects of the experiences at this age may last into adulthood. This faith is intuitive in the sense that it is filled with fantasy fed by a productive and often uninhibited and unrestrained imagination.

Children generally get their impressions of God from the adults closest to them; thus, they project images of their mother or father onto God. Although they may not say it verbally, they believe that "my daddy is God." The child can be powerfully and permanently influenced by the examples, moods, actions, and stories of the visible faith of primary related adults. The danger is that a child growing up in an abusive home may grow up with unrestrained images of terror and destruction when they think of God; or, a child that grows up in an emotionally distant family may find it difficult to comprehend any meaningful relationship with God. The potential is that positive role models and encouraged imagination can lead to a dynamic faith and expanding images of God.

This stage of faith is primarily an experienced faith. Experiencing faith through love, trust, and unconditional acceptance from primary caregivers is foundational to the development of faith. The tasks of the child in this stage are to explore and test, observe and copy, imagine and create in response to the nurturing adults in their lives. Children in this stage contribute innocence, wonder, and playfulness to a faith community.

2. Mythic-Literal Faith (elementary to adolescence)

This stage of faith is generally characteristic of children in the elementary grades of education, but it often continues into adulthood. This stage correlates with the beginning of concrete operations when children are able to narrate their own experiences and can begin to take the perspective of another. Mythic-Literal faith is a vacillating faith that works hard at differentiating between fact and fantasy, real and make-believe. A good example of this is the frequent discussions about the reality of Santa Claus. A number of years ago, when I was a staff member at a summer camp, I overheard a group of eight year-olds deliberating over this December dilemma on a hot summer day. Kids were taking sides in the debate when one wise youngster reflectively—and with some angst— replied, "Part of me says he's real and the other part of me says he's not." He went on to cite examples to prove each side of the internal debate. This child exhibited a classic stage two faith.

Which way a child-like faith vacillates probably depends on the power of the stories that have been presented to them. Children identify with the faith and values of those people important to them, and thus take the words, beliefs, attitudes, and symbols of adults very literally. Therefore they can be deeply affected by the use of symbolic and dramatic materials and can describe in endlessly detailed narrative what they have experienced. There is great potential in stories to give coherence to their experience of faith, but there is also the danger of excessive reliance on reciprocity and over-controlling perfectionism: children may perform acts of faith or religious obedience just to please a significant other. This might be reversed, without thought or reflection, when a different story is heard. As a dramatic story-teller and persuasive adult I could affect a religious act—often given ultimate salvific meaning by adults—from a child in this stage given a few minutes of their time and their undivided attention. I could turn around and have them doubt or reverse that act in a different situation a few hours later. This is why child evangelism methods should be held suspect by those who understand this stage of faith development. A personal example occurred when my spouse took our children to a children's event that was part of an evangelistic campaign in our city. My seven year-old son wanted to go forward when the invitation was given to "accept Jesus into your heart." We were quite confident that our children were being nurtured in the faith through regular Christian education at home and at church and that they would make their own decisions in God's own developmental time, and so my spouse questioned him about his motives. He replied, "I want that book they are giving away to everyone who goes down!" She promised to take him to the Christian bookstore on the way home, not wanting to pad another evangelist's statistics with child conversions done because of their desires to please adults or the lure of a free prize.

Just as this stage of faith is characteristic of children in school, it is a faith that is primarily nurtured by institutions such as the family and the church. It is an institutional faith in that it is dependent on these structures to be consistent and reliable for survival. The gift of this stage is the telling and retelling of stories. Children learn best from teachers and mentors who tell the stories of faith that will be foundational to their faith decisions in later years. My advice is that a "moral of the story," or a practical application of a story, is unnecessary and maybe even inappropriate at this stage. Rather, let the story speak for itself: let the children use their imagination, especially if it is a biblical story. These story-seeds planted in the spring-time of life will come to grow and bloom during the following stages.

Summer

3. Synthetic-Conventional Faith
(adolescence and beyond)

The transition to stage three happens when there is a contradiction of stories that leads to reflection on meanings. Faith blooms and becomes truly personal during adolescence; therefore stage three could be most accurately labelled "adolescent faith," although many continue to function in this way as adults. It begins with the ability for formal operations and abstract thinking, as well as being able to understand the perspective of another. Formal operational thinking also gives people the ability to critically compare, reflect upon, and evaluate a variety of faith stories and experiences.

This stage of faith is synthetic, not in the sense of being artificial or phony, but in the sense that it is being shaped by others—it is a relational faith. It is conventional in that a person affiliates their faith with the community they are a part of. This affiliation is expressed through attendance, participation, baptism or confirmation, or other ways to claim ownership: "I belong; therefore, I am."

One of the best examples of a synthetic conventional faith I have experienced was a girl in the youth group I led—Rhianne. Since her home life was unstable, she was always waiting at the church door when I came to set up and prepare for an evening's junior high youth group activities. She became one of the most active and loyal members of the group. I knew that our church leaders would want an account of whether the youth ministry was effective in bringing youth to faith in Christ and since my relationship with Rhianne had become quite candid, I remember one day asking her quite bluntly if she was a Christian. She said, "Yes." Being a good youth pastor who was not just interested in converts, I pursued the question a bit further: "So, how do you know you are a Christian? What makes you say that?" She looked at me as if I was the stupidest person on earth. "Well, because I belong to a Christian youth group!" My heart sank. I thought I had failed in my ministry, but as I reflected on Fowler's theory I began to see that her faith commitment was very personal, genuine, and appropriate. Rhianne was lonely, had no stability in her life, and longed to belong. There was no one she could rely on to be there for her until she met the youth and leaders at our junior high youth group. She met Jesus in that community and she began to know herself as a valued person: created in the image of God and loved unconditionally. Rhianne found somewhere to belong. Her spirituality was all about relationships and belonging.

In this stage, God is often addressed in relational terms like "friend," "guide," "defender," "mother," or "father." I recall how youth would talk about God: "God cares for me, loves me, and accepts me the way I am—God's always there for me." The analogy of faith as a personal relationship with God is very meaningful for people in this stage of faith. The gift of stage three faith is not only the awakening sense of self, but of forgiveness and acceptance of others, and loyalty to others. The potential of this relational motif is that there will be strong identification with the faith community, so this is often when baptism or confirmation takes place in the church. A sense of belonging and self-worth comes from a community that responds affirmatively, as noted in Rhianne's life.

The danger of this stage is conformity: living by the expectations of others and reaching a permanent equilibrium here. It is very common for people to get stuck in this stage, or to return to it if subsequent patterns of faith become too difficult. People become what others want them to be, depending on whom they are with or who is most influential in their lives at the time. Thus, values are often held tacitly and without much reflection or examination. Fowler believes that religious institutions work best when a majority of people are at stage three.[5] People who ask too many questions, or behave in strange ways are upsetting to the stability of the institution, even though they may be developing in faith. In my opinion, however, it is unfortunate when church life can be described as dominantly synthetic-conventional.

5. Fowler, *Stages of Faith*, 164.

Transitional Faith (emerging and young adulthood)

One of James Fowler's students, Sharon Daloz Parks, who became a scholar in her own right, theorized a separate stage of faith between Fowler's stage three and four. The transition from three to four is so significant that it can be labelled a separate stage with its own unique characteristics. Societal circumstances in the past few decades have created another developmental stage now known as emerging adulthood. The characteristics of this stage are inherently ambivalent, ideological, and transitional, which is why it is not easily recognizable as a distinct stage.[6] Jeffrey Jensen Arnett has helpfully articulated the characteristics of emerging adulthood.[7] It is an age of identity explorations—which used to be more prominent in adolescence—in response to love, work, and questions regarding ideology or worldview. It is an age of instability with the high rate of residential change being the most obvious example. It is an age of focusing on the self, with more time spent alone than any other in the lifespan except for the elderly. It is an age of feeling in-between adolescence and adulthood. And finally, it is an age of possibilities for vocational exploration and setting new directions for the future.

How does this distinct stage of life affect faith formation and spirituality? Emerging adult faith is transitioning from authority-bound faith, or unqualified relativism, to a probing commitment; from either dependence or counter-dependence on authorities to fragile inner dependence; and from conventional or diffuse groupings to self-chosen ideologically compatible groupings. This faith that is marked by transition is a searching faith that challenges, probes, questions, doubts, experiments, wonders, and wanders. It is sometimes expressed through comparison, critique, and even disagreement with its affiliating faith.

Transitional faith is marked by the discernment of vocation. Vocation is not merely our job, work, occupation, profession, or career. Our vocation may include the above, and may be a way to

6. Parks, *Critical Years*, 79–90.
7. Arnett, *Adolescence and Emerging Adulthood*, 14–15.

express our vocation, but they are not the same thing. Vocation is primarily about calling. Vocation is the response a person makes with one's total self to the calling of God for partnership in God's purposes.[8] It involves our work, play, relationships, stewardship of possessions, and private life; in other words, everything with which we serve God and our neighbour for God's purposes. The question of vocation is the primary question of young adult faith and meaning-making. The discernment of vocation is concerned with the big questions of life: Who am I? Why am I here?

The gift of transitional faith is passion: passion for asking questions, for justice, for sexuality. The danger of this stage is when this passion loses control and boundaries are crossed—resulting in addiction; promiscuity; and, ultimately pain and a wounded faith. The importance of self-chosen, ideologically compatible mentoring communities during this stage cannot be overemphasized. These communities may involve peers as well as professors and more informal intergenerational relationships.

The transition from stage three to stage four is the focus of undergraduate education, especially in faith-based institutions. This transition is like packing a bag for summer camp. When I was nine years old, heading off for my first ever week of summer camp, my mom packed my bags for me. When I turned thirteen, however, I wanted to pack my own bag. Although I may have chosen a few different items, I continued to put in shirts, pants, underwear, and socks—just as my mother would have. I also remember sneaking in a bag of sunflower seeds, simply because the camp brochure had clearly stated that we were not to bring such items. The packing of their own "faith bags" is the task of emerging adults. Whether the faith looks remarkably similar or completely different from their parents' faith is beside the point; rather, the point is that it has been packed personally through a process of reflection. As a college professor, it is sometimes my job to help a student dump their faith bag on the table to examine its contents before helping them to repack it.

8. Fowler, *Becoming Adult*, 77.

4. Individuative-Reflective Faith (adulthood)

The task of transitional faith is for faith to become wholly personal. In stage four, faith is completely owned: it is no longer the faith of parents, peers, or influential others. The process of personalizing, individualizing, or owning faith involves reflection. After a period of reflection—where faith is wary, ambivalent, and tentative—a person begins to make solid commitments to faith. Stage four faith is not often found until emerging adulthood, or more commonly, young adulthood. There has to be some interruption of external sources of authority for stage four faith to emerge; this sometimes happens when a person moves away from home, goes to college, or has an experience in another culture. In this stage, tacitly held values become explicit.

In stage four, faith takes personal responsibility for commitments, lifestyle, beliefs, and attitudes. Those in this stage of faith have doubted, questioned, compared, reflected, rejected, accepted, and decided within themselves that "this is who I am, these are my convictions, this is what I live for—wherever I am, whoever I'm with." "While others and their judgments will remain important to the individuative-reflective person, their expectations, advice and counsel will be submitted to an internal panel of experts who reserve the right to choose and who are prepared to take responsibility for their choices."[9] We can call this a first-hand faith. We often live with second-hand information regarding car repair, house renovations, or even our physical health, but when it comes to questions of meaning, purpose, and death, second-hand information will not do. "I cannot survive on a second-hand faith in a second-hand God. There has to be a personal word, a unique confrontation, if I am to come alive."[10] This is adult faith.

Although this stage of faith is labeled as individuative-reflective and is concerned with a committed interior life, the gift of adult faith is to serve others. Those who have done the inner work are able to genuinely reach out as parents to their children, or in service

9. Fowler, *Stages of Faith*, 179.
10. Peck, *Road Less Travelled*, 194.

and ministry to others in their church and community. Although the self needs to continue to be nurtured, it is natural for people at this stage to selflessly serve others. With inward stability achieved to some extent, this faith can be expressed outwardly toward others. Janet Hagberg and Robert Guelich describe faith transitions as "hitting the wall."[11] Their stages do not match up exactly with those we are using from Fowler—for example, their "wall" could describe the transition from stage three to four or from four to five—but I mention this concept here because of the importance of any transition in the growth of faith. Transitions, regardless of their exact nature, have enormous potential for spiritual formation. Just as the previous stage is generally experienced during post-secondary education in western societies, the wall between stage four and five is characteristic of the mid-life journey. This sort of wall experience may be precipitated by a significant career change, the death of a loved one, separation or divorce, an emptying nest, or a serious illness or accident. How we negotiate the wall—regardless when it occurs—will determine the future of our faith.

Autumn

Integrative Faith (mid-life)

Fowler calls this stage conjunctive faith because at this stage adults begin to make connections between all the experiences of their past. I'm calling it integrative faith because it involves the integration into the self of what was previously unrecognized—that is, reclaiming and reworking the past. This stage of faith is harvest time; here, we begin to notice some of the fruits of our adult labors as our children become adults themselves. I am presently entering this stage, although there might yet be a wall in my future.

Midlife is the autumn season; for, at the mid-point in the expected life span we are just as close to death as we are to birth. It is in midlife that for the first time, we have as much to look back on as we do to look forward to. This understanding does something

---

11. See Hagberg and Guelich, *The Critical Journey*, chapter 7.

profound to the soul. It can kill us or it can rebirth us. Our default mode is to just settle into the routines that have buoyed us for the past few decades—we sit comfortably between contentment and complacency and wish for no drastic changes in the weather.

Sometimes we think that all of our questions will be answered and life will be easier in midlife, but it is not so. In fact, the questions may increase, and new questions emerge! But we are also more content to live with the paradoxes and questions. In our younger years, we may have been driven to find answers and success, but often in midlife all that we have built up crumbles around us, or we realize that the exterior life was not all it was cracked up to be. Life made more sense when we were younger and issues were less complex. Now it is time to embrace the paradoxes and to live the unanswered questions. Unanswered questions abound in midlife but the foundation of faith remains; in fact, the questions become an integral part of our life of faith.

In the past, life was more regulated and controlled and we did not have to worry as much about our physical health. Life in our middle years may not seem as progressive as the years that were primarily focused on earning money and raising children. Sometimes the stairs we have worked so hard to ascend seem to lead to nowhere. We have experienced pain and loss and we have new questions. How will we face this second half of life? How will we process and integrate the difficult and disconcerting events of our past? How will we embrace the paradoxes—the unexplainable sufferings of the past and the unanswered questions about the future?

Winter

Universalizing Faith (an ideal)

Readers will note that infancy was also labeled with the winter season. I believe that life is in many ways circular. We came from dust, and shall return to dust. Earthly life begins when we emerge from the darkness and safety of our mother's womb and ends as we return to the darkness and safety of death—the womb of God. The Bible uses a lot of death and life, and rebirth language, and I believe that life is reborn in another dimension at death. What is death, and life-after-death like? Life on earth is mysterious enough, but the concept of eternal life in other dimensions is incomprehensible.

As we move into the winter of life, we become more aware of the reality of our death and the limitations of our mind and body. It can be depressing to look back and see life vigorous and exciting, and then to look ahead and see a crumbling body, and eventually death. Although there is always a fear of death as we contemplate its mystery, there is also a contentedness in realizing that since there is nothing we can do to reverse the journey, we can savour and enjoy each moment more fully.

This stage, in Fowler's model, seems to be an ideal endpoint. Fowler lists modern heroes or saints of faith such as Ghandi and Mother Theresa as examples of universalizing faith. Perhaps the best way to summarize this endpoint is to let Fowler's eloquent language speak for itself:

> Beyond paradox and polarities, persons in this stage are grounded in a oneness with the power of their being. Their visions and commitments free them for a passionate yet detached spending of the self in love, devoted to overcoming division, oppression, and violence, and in effective anticipatory responses to the imminent in-breaking of the commonwealth of love and justice.

Pelagius wisely said, "The young person serves others with his mind and body; the old person serves others with his soul."[12] The wisdom of the soul is the gift of people in their later years. They are closest to God in the circle of life. Let us sit at their feet and glean from that closeness.

12. As quoted in Newel, *One Foot in Eden*, 77.

For Reflection

Which season of life are you in at present?

How do you identify or not identify with the
description of that season in this chapter?

Are you restless or content in that season? Why?

Are you in the midst of a transition or "hitting a wall"?
What is this like?

What developmental tasks await you in your continued
spiritual formation?

7

Hand Me Downs:
Family Systems and Faith

I REMEMBER WHEN HAND-ME-DOWN clothes were a curse; something freely given that we wished would be given to someone else. Now, they have become a commodity, something people pay for. Second hand stores like Value Village, Good Will, and MCC Thrift Stores have become hot shopping destinations for teens and young adults in search of fashions. Vintage clothing websites abound. Growing up as the eldest child in the family, I was at an advantage when it came to hand-me-downs, but I would dread the day my mother would come home from a distant relative's house with "new" clothing for me. What I didn't get in hand-me-downs my mother would sew for me so I was the proudest young adolescent when I got my first pair of new blue jeans from the Sears catalogue, complete with little Canadian flags embroidered on the front pockets. No more second hand polyester for me! I wanted my own clothing.

As we have seen in the previous chapter, the personalizing and owning of our faith is an important quality of spirituality; however, we cannot avoid being shaped by our family of origin. Today, there are many different types of families besides the North American stereotype of Mom, Dad, and two children. Regardless of what kind of parents Mom and/or Dad were and are or what kind of faith or lack of faith they had, or what kind of family structure one has been part of, the family unit is the primary shaper of faith; "primary" meaning the first as well as the principal shaper of faith. Not only does our family provide the content and form of our faith but the structure of it as well. "For better or worse, whether intentionally or haphazardly, it is within these 'given' families that, as children, our hearts and minds are fundamentally formed. Here we develop a sense of identity and heritage; here we learn patterns of relating intimately with others; here we hammer out our values, ideals, and habits day by day and year by year."[1] The family plays a vital role in handing down aspects of our faith.

The Bible doesn't really give a lot of prescriptions or advice about the proper structure of the family, but what it does say is important for us to consider. First of all, the family is the foundation for human society as well as for local communities.[2] Thus, the family is also the central institution for living and passing on the faith. It is important to note that the focus in the Bible is more on family relationships than family structure. There are very few traditional nuclear families but a lot of blended, extended, broken, dysfunctional, and troubled families in the Bible. The nuclear "focus on the family" ideal is more a product of North American middle class values than of biblical values. In the Bible, identity, and even spiritual identity, was tied to family ancestry. The early church spread primarily through family systems and households and most often met in family homes. Yet, at the same time as these positive family values in Scripture, there is also often tension between family and faith.[3]

Thus, the biblical view of family is very relevant for our day; in that families continue to be foundational, there are increasing varieties of family structures, and despite—or sometimes be-cause of religious pluralism—tensions of faith exist that are most acutely felt in families.

1. Thompson, *Family*, 19–20.
2. Genesis 2:18–24.
3. Luke 14:26; Mark 3:31–35.

Family Systems

I would like to combine family systems theory with spiritual formation. It seems to me that family systems have a profound influence on how we express our faith as adults. I am not aware of any previous research that combines family systems theory and religious development. My proposal is based on a combination of my research into family systems theory; the process of spiritual formation; many years of ministry with youth, young adults, and their parents. I have presented this material to college classes for more than five years now and students have experienced numerous "aha!" moments as they begin to understand their family system and how it may have shaped the way they express their faith. It has helped me to understand the family system of my own family of origin and how it has shaped me.

Before we look at the model, we must understand a few preliminary assumptions. First of all, that the family is indeed a system. "A family is not merely a collection of separate individuals who happen to share the same last name and street address. It is an organism, in which the attitudes, values, and actions of each member interact with those of all the other members."[4] Although parents are the most influential factor, children—and possibly extended family members as well—also influence the others in the family. Because relationships are complex, the influence here is multi-directional: it is a system that is interactive and often triangular rather than linear. My theory is that our faith behaviors, beliefs, and feelings of belonging—whether healthy or unhealthy—will flow from the roles we occupy in our particular family system.

The second assumption is that family systems are generally resistant to change. This is called *homeostasis*, which means "of the same status," or the tendency to stay the same regardless of circumstances; like how our body temperature adjusts to stay stable at about 37 degrees Celsius regardless of the air temperature. There is a kind of inertia to family systems that make them tend to keep going the way they always have despite negativity or danger.

4. Stoop, *Forgiving our Parents*, 50.

In families, a pattern of relationships is established in which everyone is assigned a role and powerful forces within the system work to keep things the same even if circumstances change. Different members also reinforce one another in their roles, attitudes, and actions in order to keep things the same. Family secrets that everyone knows about but leaves unaddressed—such as incest, alcoholism, or abuse—and family myths that everyone talks about but no one acts upon—such as a sense of family closeness—also reinforce the family system.

In case you are getting discouraged by now, a third assumption is that a healthy family system is possible. A healthy, well-adjusted family is adaptable to change and has positive attachments to one another. They are balanced between being close and being separate and between stability and flexibility. David Stoop lists three basic ingredients of a well-adjusted family:[5] 1) Mutual respect that expresses itself in a tolerance (even appreciation) for differences. 2) Respect for members of other generations and resourceful connections with them. 3) People are free to experience their own emptiness without others trying to fix or judge them.

How do we understand the influence of family systems on the development of faith? I think the following matrix of family systems can give us some help. The psychologists at Minirth-Meier Clinic have developed a theory of family systems based on two scales: attachment and adaptability. These scales have resulted in six basic family systems which I have applied to faith and developed it into a four-fold matrix with a fifth ideal family that is both adaptable and attached, and exhibits a faith that is growing and holistic, relational and flexible. It is important to consider that the four-fold matrix creates four extreme caricatures and an idealistic fifth one. [6] Most families will probably have a tendency toward one of the four, but the faith of most members of Christian families will hopefully also fall "within the cross" and be basically healthy with some possible characteristics of un-health. As with other models

5. Ibid., 74–75.

6. See table on page 79: "Family Systems and Faith: a hypothetical matrix based on family systems theory."

describing faith, no one model captures things completely and accurately.

Six Types of Family Systems on Two Axes[7]

I. Adaptability is how well the family adjusts or adapts to change and how well a family deals with problems that come up.

1. Rigid Family:

Rigid families tend to make decisions quickly and arbitrarily and then impose them on family members. They tend not to allow the expression of emotions or tend to ignore them if they are expressed, resulting in a buildup of anger that is often expressed in indirect and manipulative ways. Rigid families generally have authoritarian, clearly defined leadership roles with strict and non-negotiable rules. When rules are broken the punishment is often swift and stern.

2. Chaotic Family:

Chaotic families, on the other extreme, express a lot of emotion but it all gets lost in the shuffle. The resulting impulsiveness often stirs up anger. Chaotic families may take a great deal of time talking through issues, but in a confused and disorganized way—possibly never really arriving at a clear decision. There is probably no visible leadership, so each individual is on their own and authority shifts from one to another sporadically and spontaneously. In a chaotic family, rules are unwritten, unspoken, and changeable. Decisions are never really made and stuff just happens.

---

7. See appendix 2 for a personal family systems inventory to help place your family of origin.

3. Adaptable Family:

A healthy family lies in between these two extremes. An adaptable family has clear but flexible leadership that is willing to listen to others in the family. The methods of discipline are fair and adjustable to circumstances. Problems are discussed and the discussions lead to decisions that reflect the input of various members. In adaptable families the roles are clear: parents are parents, children are children, but communication is plentiful.

II. Attachment is how family members bond with one another and how they relate to each other.

4. Disengaged Family:

The disengaged family experiences a complete lack of emotional bonding within the family unit. They do not experience a lot of togetherness or closeness; instead, they value independence and relationships outside the family. Boundaries within the family system are strictly enforced but outside they are flexible or nonexistent, which may leave family members feeling isolated from each other. They probably do not spend a lot of meaningful time together as a family.

5. Enmeshed Family:

The enmeshed family is at the other end of the spectrum—they have an extreme sense of closeness and loyalty bordering on closed-ness to those outside the family. Independence or separateness is seen as disloyalty to the family; consequently, everything is everybody else's business. Since there are very few family boundaries inside the system, this family may look very close and attractive from the outside, but it may leave members on the inside feeling suffocated.

6. Attached Family:

The family that has healthy attachments gives members a sense of individuality as well as connectedness to each other. They enjoy being together but give each other space to be active outside of family as well. The healthy attached family shows support for individual uniqueness as well as appreciation for outside accomplishments.

Each family falls somewhere on the axis of adaptability and the axis of attachment to create the four-fold matrix with an ideal fifth. See appendix 2 for an inventory of questions to help you discern the family system of your family of origin.

Family Systems and Faith

What kind of spirituality might result from each of these types of families? How would each one attempt to pass on faith to the next generation? How might they address God in prayer and worship? I have developed five caricatures, and my hypothesis is that every family will probably tend towards one of these. I am using Christian language and examples but I believe it could be applied to any religion or those with no religion. Identifying our family's tendency will hopefully help each of us begin to deal with the kinds of faith that have been handed down to us by our families.

Family Systems and Faith: A hypothetical matrix based on family systems theory

Chaotic Family	Cold Faith		Casual Faith
Adaptable Family		Growing Relational Faith	
Rigid Family	Controlled Faith		Co-depen-dent Faith
ADAPTABILITY ↑ ATTACHMENT →	Disengaged Family	Attached Family	Enmeshed Family

A **controlled faith** will likely be the result of someone who grew up in a rigid and disengaged family. Following the rules and living uprightly will be a more important value than the cultivation of relationships. Faith will be seen as being primarily about obedience to the teaching of the Bible and living a life of moral purity. The Bible is seen as inerrant and infallible and clearly outlines non-negotiable roles and rules which are to be obeyed. Questioning these rules or questioning the family authority who is teaching them would be seen as sin and rebellion. God would be primarily seen as the ultimate authority: almighty, all-knowing, and unchanging; and might be primarily addressed as Father, Judge, King, or Lord. My guess is that this caricature of faith is most typical of people raised in traditional, conservative, fundamentalist evangelical homes, especially those of a generation ago.

What I call a **cold faith** will be the fruit of a chaotic and disengaged family. This kind of family does not believe in pushing religion down anyone's throat, so to speak. Consequently, it will seem like everybody for themselves as far as faith goes. There is no religious instruction, moral guidance, or spiritual formation activity in this family. Each person can decide on their own if they want to have faith or what faith they want to commit themselves to. Spirituality is about individual freedom: a private compartmentalized thing that cannot and should not be taught. If there is a God, this God is whoever you conceive him/it/her to be, and God is not really addressed personally. From my perspective, someone growing up in this kind of home is growing up in a faith vacuum. My hunch is that this kind of spirituality would be most typical of those who grew up in a completely secular, nonreligious family system, perhaps in reaction against the previous one.

A **co-dependent faith** would most likely result from a rigid and enmeshed family system. These kinds of families are very close to each other and closed to outside influences. They value the unique relationships and rules within the family unit. Faith is passed down by parents, elders, or family-endorsed mentors in controlled relationships. Faith is part of the extended family culture and the church or any particular religious group will be seen as an extension of the family; or, the church may be made up of extended family members. Faith is about loyalty and conformity to the community. God will be addressed as a personal Savior, protector, and defender—a kind of local deity. Loyalty to God, family, and church are almost the same thing. Ethnic minorities, immigrants, and those raised in a home school environment might tend toward this kind of spiritual formation.

This type of faith is particularly poignant for my own background. Mennonites, persecuted because of their radical dissociation with the state church in the sixteenth century, became an ethnic minority group within a few generations, moving eastward in Europe in attempts to maintain their faith. The original name of my particular church in early nineteenth century Russia was *Kleine Gemeinde*, which means "small church;" derisively given but proudly embraced because they wanted to be the faithful remnant of God's people, away from the larger Mennonite church which they felt had gone astray—the rest of the world was not even on their radar at the time. Even though I am a fourth generation Canadian, my family was still a minority where Mennonite faith, family, and ethnicity were often one and the same. While I was growing up, people who did not come to our church and did not have a "Mennonite name" were outsiders often viewed with suspicion. Many other conservative Mennonite groups such as the Amish or Old Colony would have a similar background of faith.

This was combined in my generation with the influence of North American evangelical revivalism on my denomination; however, because of the particular dynamics in my family—with a strong, nurturing, and open-minded mother whose extended family were a significant part of the congregation—my family of origin primarily functioned in the codependent mode rather than in the controlled faith more typical of families in the evangelical tradition.

A **casual faith** will probably be the result of a chaotic enmeshed family system. In this family system, relationships are everything, where rules and dogmas are seen to come between people and restrict their relationships with God. God's unconditional love, grace, and mercy will be highly valued and God will be worshiped as Creator and Lover with a particular emphasis on Jesus as Friend. The essence of faith is living in harmony with all people, being inclusive, and being able to express oneself openly and emotionally if desired. A relationship with God should happen naturally without coercion or reliance on religious dogma or ritual. I think this tendency toward a casual faith might be typical of some charismatic groups coming out of the Jesus movement in the 1960s, some mainline denominations, and even some emergent evangelical groups who are reacting to their rigid and disengaged background. The spate of books and YouTube rants about loving Jesus and not religion are examples of this kind of faith.

My closing comments about typical examples for each type are anecdotal and need to be taken with a grain of salt, but I do think that not only family systems, but the church systems those families participate in contribute to the shape of participants' spirituality.

	Family "Mantra"	Conception of God	Faith Formation	Spirituality
Rigid and disengaged family	"rules before relationships"	Father Authority	Teaching obedience	Controlled Moral purity
Chaotic and disengaged family	"everyone for themselves"	Whatever you conceive	On your own	Cold Private and detached
Rigid and enmeshed family	"close and closed"	Personal Saviour	Endorsed mentors	Co-dependent Loyalty to community
Chaotic and enmeshed family	"relationships are everything"	Unconditional acceptance	Unstructured relationships	Casual Inclusive harmony
Adaptable and attached Family	"roots and wings"	Love and Justice	Inter-generational relationships	Growing relationship

The faith of those raised in adaptable and attached families will hopefully be a **growing and relational faith.** This is the ideal nurturing environment that all Christian families strive for: a balanced family life that gives children both well-grounded spiritual roots as well as wings to explore their faith. These families value foundational biblical principles but are open to discussion and questioning as a necessary part of growth. Faith is, first of all, a right relationship with God and with others, followed by right belief and moral behavior. Thus, God is seen as embracing both unconditional love and passionate justice. Faith is best passed on through healthy relationships between generations that include mentors and guides other than a child's parents. Spiritual formation does not just happen; rather, it is something that needs to be worked at deliberately and thoughtfully. May all our families be like this!

Unfortunately, not all families are like this and all families will probably have a tendency toward one of the other types. It will help us to know and understand our own spirituality by examining what has been handed down to us by our families of origin. It does not mean we are locked in for life—sometimes we will react by going to the opposite extreme—but it does mean we have some reflecting and processing to do on our journey of faith.

For Reflection

How has your family shaped your faith? How does this evidence itself presently?

Which family system does your family of origin have a tendency towards? Why? What kind of faith has resulted in different members of your family?

What work is there for you to do to process your family's influence?

8

Period Costumes: The Influence of Historical Movements

ONE OF MY SONS is fascinated with the history, literature, and fashion of medieval Europe. For his graduation suit we went to a small, out of the way medieval and gothic clothing store where he chose a billowing white frilly shirt, a deep red paisley vest, and a greatcoat in bold paisley black fastened with hooks and eyes. Some slim black slacks with a pair of large-buckle shoes, and a cane for his accessory rounded out his period costume. He was dashing! A few years later, when we were in London together, we attended a performance of Shakespeare at the Globe Theatre. The authentic period architecture, seating, and costumes added much to the performance.

People have dressed differently, for cultural and practical reasons, in different periods of history. History may not be on everyone's favorite subject list, but I dare say its study has much relevance for us today. But why have a chapter on history in a book about spirituality? Faith is not only handed down from our families of origin, it can be traced back in history to a myriad of movements hundreds of years ago. There are over two thousand years of Christian history, after all! Historical expressions of spirituality and ways of practising faith have shaped the way we express ourselves and the way we nurture faith today. The better we know the spiritual traditions that have influenced us, the deeper our own journey of spiritual formation can be, and the more meaningfully we can travel with others.

Countless books have been written about the different spiritual traditions that exist today, never mind reading all the classic writings themselves. I appreciate how Richard Foster traces six spiritual streams throughout Christian history.[1] Each one emphasizes a particular practice of Christian living that, taken together, gives us a holistic view of spirituality. The Contemplative stream values prayer, the Holiness tradition emphasizes virtuous living, the Charismatic stream emphasizes spiritual empowerment, the Social Justice way focuses on compassionate living, the Evangelical stream emphasizes scriptural guidance, and the Incarnational stream focuses on the sacramental aspect of daily living.

For our purposes, I will be choosing three specific historical movements that fit into a number of the streams mentioned in Foster's book. These movements are ones that have and are influencing our present spirituality in North America: the Celtic spirituality of the western European hinterlands in the fifth and sixth centuries, the Anabaptist movement of continental Europe in the sixteenth century, and the Awakenings of evangelical revivalism in North America in the eighteenth and nineteenth centuries.

Why look at these three particular spiritual traditions? All three of them have shaped the spiritualties of significant numbers of Christians in North America today—in particular, evangelical revivalism, which has shaped Christian spirituality on the entire continent. There is currently a resurgent interest in Anabaptism and Celtic spirituality, even among people who have no direct historical connection to the original movements. As Christendom has crumbled in Europe, and is crumbling in North America, there is new interest in fringe movements like these that went against the prevailing model of Christianity at the times of their origins. All three of them, in the past and the present, attempt to get back to the roots of what it means to follow Christ, which provides hope for us in a time of spiritual uncertainty.

1. Foster, *Streams of Living Water.*

Awakening Spirituality

The evangelical Awakenings have had a pervasive influence on North American Christian spirituality. When we look at the spirituality of the Awakenings we could span a time period from the 1700s to 1946, though our primary focus will be on what is called the "Second Awakening" from about 1776 to 1846. The industrial revolution and the First Awakening will form the backdrop and the period after will provide us with some of the institutions that resulted from the movement. I will be focussing on the youthfulness of the movement because I believe that it is often the young who lead us in renewal and change.

The industrial revolution was a time marked by rapid and often violent change. It was an age of transition. Youth were in the middle of it in both Europe and North America. Not only did the population increase dramatically in this era, but in 1840 70 percent of the population in North America was under thirty—today this is reversed—and the median age was sixteen—today this has doubled! This growing mass of young people was looked at in two contrasting ways: some saw it as a huge societal problem and some saw its immense potential. There were also significant economic changes going on as the western world saw a move from a feudal-landowner agricultural society to an industrialized, urbanized, and capitalized economy. It became economically advantageous to create an abundance of wage labor so many youth migrated from farms and domestic industries to the cities and factory towns. There were social changes as well: peer groups became increasingly important in urban areas as young men did not have family supports available. Leisure activities became more public: dancing, sleigh rides, card playing, and walking (i.e. courtship). Social groups were separated according to social class: unemployed laborers formed neighborhood gangs and wealthier students dabbled with bohemianism, causing much turmoil on American college campuses.

This tumultuous time of upheaval and change seemed ripe for spiritual awakening. While German pietism yielded the "Order of the Grain of Mustard Seed" and the beginning of the Moravian missionary movement, and English Methodism produced the "Holy Club of Oxford" and the abolitionist movement, Jonathan Edwards and George Whitefield were leading massive evangelical revivals on campuses and in churches of the Thirteen Colonies. Out of these movements of the first Great Awakening came many institutions that are still thriving today: numerous denominations from Evangelical Lutherans to Southern Baptists, YMCA, Sunday School, and many missionary organizations, Christian publishing companies, youth organizations, and even the political formation of USA and Canada. But how did all this tumult, change, and religious organizing shape the spirituality of much of North America for generations to come? What did this spirituality look like? Finding out may give us some insights into our own spirituality today.

During the Second Awakening, revivals often began in Christian societies on campus and spread to local church revivals that consisted mainly of the conversion of young people. "It was through the evangelical revivals of the eighteenth and nineteenth centuries that countless youth found support and a sense of direction that their background and situation could not provide. As the new century began, public expectations of youth had never been higher, yet there was probably no period since the late eighteenth century when there were more complaints about youthful misconduct."[2]

Because of the revivals, adolescence was seen as a universal time of religious and sexual awakening often with blurred lines between the two (Rob Bell's *SexGod* is not a new idea). This gave birth to modern psychology, with G. Stanley Hall's theory labelling adolescence as a time of "storm and stress," characterized by oscillations between extremes of emotions and behaviors.

The spirituality of this era was indeed marked by an emotional and experiential faith, sometimes referred to as pietism—a response to unfeeling German Scholasticism, Anglican stiffness, and American pragmatism. This more personal spirituality included bodily manifestations, healing, dancing, falling, shouting, weeping, and laughing, or as Jonathan Edwards says, "Affections

---

2. Gillis, *Youth and History*, 80.

are very great or raised very high . . . [there are] great effects on the body . . . [and most importantly] evangelical humiliation."[3]

Part of the emotional experience during the revivals was a dramatic conversion experience. Conversion was an event that each person had to experience to be genuinely saved. This experience often involved a public act such as coming forward at a meeting—again accompanied by great emotion and prayers of repentance acknowledging sin and turning to a new moral life. Youth was seen as the primary period for conversion and a majority of the converts during the Second Awakening were teenagers and young adults.

Most of these conversions happened at mass gatherings which began in the late nineteenth century with camp meetings and tent revivals that accompanied westward expansion of the colonies. In the twentieth century, these meetings were transformed into stadium rallies in urban centres. Baptists and Methodists dominated the Second Awakening after the Presbyterians had dominated the First Awakening. Charles Finney was the most famous preacher of this era. He developed a careful method of holding a revival meeting—a method that borders on manipulation, in my opinion, but to him was simply "breaking up fallow ground to prepare for the seed of the Word." His methods included the "anxious bench," the "altar call," and the calling out of names in the audience. Many others continue to use similar methods to this day. It has become part of our spiritual formation practice.

The conversion experienced was accompanied by "follow-up" activities that included methodological Bible study—where Methodists get their name—and the encouragement to attend church, pray regularly, and live uprightly. This emphasis on personal piety and holiness with a scorn for the world birthed the temperance movement, the publication of Christian literature and curriculum, and eventually Christian youth organizations.

Awakening spirituality was also an awakening to the plight of the world: the poor and the lost. Many young people sacrificed greatly as they left everything for a cause, whether it was moral,

3. Edwards, *Concerning the Religious Affections*, 127–142.

evangelistic, social, political, or missional. Many independent faith mission organizations were born as a result. The motto of the Student Volunteer Movement led by DL Moody and John R. Mott was, "The evangelization of the world in this generation" and many young people sought to bring it to fruition by going overseas or getting involved at home. Accompanying evangelism and missions was an emphasis on social reform on behalf of the poor. The Social Gospel movement—separate, but related—worked for temperance, the abolition of slavery, and women's suffrage, and in Canada eventually helped to produce universal health care.

Perhaps most remarkably, the energy of this movement fuelled the movement towards independence and nationalism on both sides of the border—in the eighteenth century in USA and the nineteenth in Canada. Although stronger in USA, there were movements in both countries to develop a national Christian religion where the line between commitment to God and country was often blurred. This continued into the war-dominated twentieth century when Christian youth were pressured to conform for the public good in the fight against the so-called evil in Eastern Europe. The Second World War created a crusading spirit among the young men who returned from the war. They had rid the world of the fascist and imperialist threats of Germany and Japan and they returned home with the belief that they had saved the world. Now they would lead in another crusade—the campaign to change the spiritual convictions of the nation at home.

This has been a very brief sweep of North American evangelical spirituality in the past century. For good or ill, directly or indirectly, we have all been touched.[4]

Anabaptist Spirituality

I trace my spiritual heritage back to the Anabaptist movement of the sixteenth century, and I became a convinced Anabaptist as a reporter for a leftist student newspaper at Brandon University in the

4. For further reading see Cairns, *An Endless Line of Splendor*; Weisberger, *They Gathered at the River*.

twentieth. When I took Anabaptist History at a Mennonite college I was intrigued by the radical nature of my spiritual ancestors, but at university I began to see the relevance of their convictions for myself and for the contemporary issues of the world. As a news reporter I was exposed in a new way to political issues on campus, in our city, and in the world. When my colleagues on the newspaper staff found out that I was a Mennonite, I received a deep respect from them because they knew about my pacifist commitments while many of my evangelical Christian friends were ridiculed as right-wing war-mongers. This gave me pause to reflect on and appreciate my faith heritage in a new way as I had the opportunity to describe the person and message of Jesus in a way that was refreshing even to me in the telling! I had always been apologetic about being Mennonite growing up, and was very reluctant to join the church, but here I was coming full circle and embracing my spiritual heritage as I gave witness to my faith. Now, I teach a course on Anabaptist History and Thought with enthusiasm!

I believe that the Anabaptist spiritual tradition has a unique and significant voice in the contemporary milieu of postmodernism because of its inherent distrust of Christendom Christianity, and because of its willingness to embrace—and even push—the radical margins of Christian theology and church. This is why many in the British Commonwealth are discovering the value of this movement for the church in the era of post-Christendom even though they have no direct historical connections.[5] The rediscovery of this tradition is having a shaping impact on many people today, whether they have a personal history in this tradition or not.

Arnold Snyder was really the first historian to examine Anabaptist spirituality instead of history, theology, culture, and ethics which had been dealt with extensively before. He proposed that Anabaptist spirituality of the sixteenth century could be

---

5. See Murray, *The Naked Anabaptist*. Murray's "seven core convictions" attempt to make Anabaptism relevant to the issues facing a post-Christendom society in the UK, but it has also generated interest in North America where the fall of Christendom is not far behind.

summarized in one German word, *gelassenheit*, which is loosely translated as "yieldedness" or "surrender."[6]

The Christian is yielded, first of all, to the Spirit. The Holy Spirit gives birth to a new person as one repents or yields, but this new birth is by God's power and not by faith alone. The emphasis was on the experience of the Spirit of Christ within rather than on the historically imputed work of Christ as other Reformers tended to emphasize.

In response to the birth of the Spirit, the person then yields to water baptism. Water baptism was a public display of commitment to Christ and to the church. It symbolized death to the old life, the outpouring of the Spirit, and the rising to a new life of discipleship. Water baptism for adult believers became the thing that gave the Anabaptists their name and marked them as separate from the prevailing Christian empire.

Water baptism was not merely an inward yieldedness of the individual but also had a communal dimension: yieldedness to the church. Surrendering to each other in the body of Christ meant yielding to discipline and the ban, because the Spirit not only renews individuals but brings them together in a mutually accountable community.

Yieldedness also meant submission to the way of Christ—the way of love and non-resistance. Christians are to imitate Christ in the way of peace: taking up the cross and not the sword of revenge. The way of Christ also included giving up and sharing temporal and material goods for the sake of the community of Christ.[7]

Finally and ultimately, the follower of Christ is called to take up the cross of martyrdom. The Christian life is all or nothing—ultimate *gelassenheit* is giving your life for the cause of Christ—and so martyrdom became a central part of Anabaptist spirituality.[8]

The Anabaptist movement of the sixteenth century was in many respects a radical youth movement. History has often made

6. Snyder, *Following in the Footsteps.*

7. This was most rigorously practiced by the Hutterite Anabaptists in the 16th century and still today.

8. See York, *The Purple Crown.*

its leaders appear older than they were, while their own contemporaries often despised their youth. Many of the first generation of leaders were young radical intellectuals who were dead before they reached the age of thirty, yet are now revered as founders of the movement. What kind of spirituality would we find if we examined a few personal writings of young Anabaptists? By looking at three sixteenth century documents by Conrad Grebel, aged twenty-two to twenty-five; Nelleken Jaspers, aged nineteen; and Hans Denck, aged twenty-five to twenty-six we will find a unique snapshot of a youthful Anabaptist spirituality.[9] Young people today are looking for a spirituality that is not afraid to confront and engage the prevailing culture as did these three almost five hundred years ago.

The first quality that runs through each of their personal documents is a sense of authenticity. They bare their souls about their faith and do not mince their words as they describe their spiritual passions. They could be described as having a bit of an edge, appearing almost cocky and rebellious in their faith. They were strong-willed, emotive, and passionate about their idealistic convictions even though they all seemed to be aware of the possible cost. Despite their firm commitments and counting the cost as individuals, they all had strong communal bonds and felt support from their faith friends and community. Perhaps it was the presence of such a community that fostered this passionate individual commitment. They all shared a deep trust in the leading of the Spirit and displayed significant knowledge of and dependence on the Scriptures.

The spirit of these three young radicals made an impact on me as a young adult forming my spiritual identity. The movement as a whole has made an impact much wider than on the relatively small number of people belonging to Mennonite and Brethren in Christ congregations in North America and around the world. The emphases on following Christ in all of life, the importance

9. See the Grebel letters in Harder, *Sources of Swiss Anabaptism*, 106–322; for Hans Denck see Fellman, *Selected Writings*, 99–119. My paraphrase of Nelleken Jasper's letter in Martyr's Mirror is included in appendix 3.

of community, and the stand for the way of peace, have become priorities for many Christians of all persuasions.[10]

Celtic Spirituality

Although Celtic spirituality is the oldest of the three chronologically, it has only recently become widely known and celebrated. Historical records about the Celts are scant and scattered and include much legend. Historically, "Celtic" refers to a linguistic cultural group mostly residing in Ireland, Wales, and the western islands of Scotland that took up residence in these areas before the time of Christ. Christianity came to these lands in the second century along with the spread of the Roman Empire. The Roman Empire withdrew from these areas in the fourth and fifth centuries, coincidentally the same era as the Christianization of the Empire took place. The islands were subsequently settled by Germanic tribes, primarily the Anglo-Saxons from across the North Sea. Christianity, with limited structures, appears to have survived the transitions. Patrick (387–460) was instrumental in making Christianity the religion of the majority—legends abound about how this transpired. What is clear is that a distinct and often marginalized version of Christian spirituality was the result. Brigit of Kildare (451–525) is the female saint associated with Celtic Christianity.

The Roman-centred faith and organization on the continent had less effect on these hinterlands it seems. Here, Christianity primarily followed local and tribal culture. The island of Iona became central to the collection and spread of Celtic Christianity.[11] The monastery established there by Columba (521–597), who came from Ireland, became a central place for spiritual formation, education, missionary work, and spiritual pilgrimage.

10. Many well known authors and thinkers have identified with these core Anabaptist values: Brian McLaren, Tony Campolo, Stuart Murray, and Stanley Hauerwas to name a few.

11. See Powers, *The Celtic Quest*, for more information about the history and contemporary relevance of Celtic spirituality.

Celtic Spirituality was dominated by monasticism and its ascetic, communal lifestyle; it developed its own poetry, writing, art, and oral traditions. Celtic spirituality was characterized by the use of the local and tribal vernaculars in liturgy in addition to Latin, and private soul friends in addition to clergy. It became in later years anti-hierarchical, independent, and nonconformist in spirit against both Roman Catholic and Anglican elitism. Celtic spirituality attempted to be a local, enculturated Christianity. And because it was on the fringes of an empire it was characterized by martyrdom: if not shedding blood for Christ literally at least doing penance or going on pilgrimage as a sign of separation from the world and commitment to Christ. With its local emphasis and its location at the edge of the continent came a focus on the created world. The Celts embraced all of creation, including a special reverence for certain birds, a focus on physical place and holy sites, and an embracing of the human body.

There was much contact and cross-influence with Saxon and Roman culture, making it difficult to distinguish what is unique in subsequent centuries. Other characteristics of what we know today as Celtic Spirituality were added and developed in subsequent years based on early traditions and writings. The Irish, Welsh, and Scots came to North America with other settlers from the British Isles, but it was English dissident groups such as the Congregationalists, Puritans, Methodists, and Baptists that dominated the formation of the American colonies. The present resurgence of interest in Celtic spirituality has skipped many generations. Today, it is the reverence for creation and sacred place, localism, nonconformity, and community that attracts attention. The worship resources of the Iona community are widely known, utilized, and appreciated all over the world and many people from North America make pilgrimage to the Isle of Iona (including myself).[12]

Although Celtic spirituality developed on the fringes of a more dominant stream of Christianity, its rich history and contemporary relevance have contributed to its resurgence and increasing influence today.

12. See www.iona.org.uk for more information about the Iona community.

All three of these movements sought to restore the essence of biblical faith and the Jesus way of life. They have all shaped the spirituality of many people in North America, and the latter two are making a resurgence of impact beyond their small numbers.

For Reflection

What do all three streams of Christian spirituality have in common? What significant differences do you note between them?

Which of these movements has been most influential in your life? How have you been influenced by each one of these movements? How might you begin to process these influences toward growth in your life?

Which one would you like to explore in more depth for future influence?

9

The Latest Fashion: Spirituality
in a Changing Culture

IT IS HARD TO keep up with the latest fashions (to be honest, I do not even try). The one good thing about clothing styles is that if you keep them long enough they are sure to be in fashion again soon! Another thing I have observed about fashions today is that there really is not one fashionable look. When I was growing up people were ridiculed if they wore unfashionable clothing, such as the plaid polyester pants I was forced to wear, but today people can dress as oddly as they want and there is always somebody more extreme. All styles of clothing seem to be acceptable and I think this is a good thing. Different styles may put you in a particular social demographic, but everyone seems to belong somewhere. This variety is part of the culture we live in.

The culture that we live in affects our spirituality—and I hope you understand that this is an understatement. I am not an anthropologist or missiologist so I will only briefly mention an interesting observation about the influences of continental cultures and leave the local cultures and ethnicities throughout the world to others who are more knowledgeable. I've heard that passion and expression characterizes Latin American spirituality, community characterizes the spirituality of African and Aboriginal cultures, thoughtful and sometimes mystical contemplation is typical of Asian spirituality, while actions and dogmas are an important part of European and western spirituality. Have you experienced any of these to be true? In the twenty-first century we are developing a global culture where some of these idiosyncrasies may be fading. Particularly in North American and western societies we are being influenced by post-modernism. It is the latest fashion.

Culture Shifts

There are many ways to define and discuss the effects of our wider culture on the formation of our spirituality. "Post" modernism assumes that this thing called postmodernism is tied to modernism. There is argument about whether postmodernism is the last death throes of modernism or whether it is actually something new. You can make up your mind on that for yourself because for our casual study it is not of utmost importance. There is also disagreement about whether postmodern culture is an opportunity to embrace or a threat to avoid for spiritual formation. Again, careful discernment is necessary, and I would say it is probably a bit of both: there are aspects to embrace and others to be wary of. The important thing for us will be to understand postmodernism as our present philosophical and cultural reality, and then to understand how it affects our spirituality. I will briefly compare postmodernism with modernism in four areas.[1]

Modernism has a scientific and material view of the universe; that is, ultimate reality is what can be observed with our senses. We could call this a closed universe where God or other spiritual forces are not part of the picture. This, of course, is a reaction to "pre-modernism," where everything that happened was attributed to God or gods. Over the past century, materialism and secularism have been shown to be seriously lacking in helping human beings cope with the world. Postmodernism has reacted to modernism with a more open view of the universe that has more room for mystery.

A second comparison involves the definition of truth. Modernism sees truth as something objective that can be proven or

---

1. See Erickson, *Postmodernizing the Faith*, 16–19; Tony Jones, *Postmodern Youth Ministry*, 30–37; McLaren, *A New Kind of Christian*, 11–38 for similar comparative lists.

disproven through the scientific method or rational logic. Conse-quently, what can be proven as true is true absolutely and univer-sally. Postmodernism doubts any certainty and so truth is whatever one chooses; that is, what is true is only true locally. Something must be personally experienced to be true, so what is true for you may not be true for me. In this system, minority voices are valued as much—or more—as powerful majority voices.

Thirdly, modernism trumpets the dignity and importance of the individual. Modern philosopher, Rene Descartes, said in prototypical modern fashion, "I think therefore I am." Modern psychologist, Abraham Maslow, proposes that meaning comes from self-actualization. However, the "I" has become lonely and longs for community, and so the postmodern philosopher sings, "I want somewhere to belong."[2] Meaning comes from belonging in a tribe or community.

Finally, modernism is optimistic and focuses on progress. For this reason, the twentieth century could be characterized as both the climax and the downfall of modernism. It saw the formation of many new countries, the invention of the automobile, the first person in space, the invention of the computer and the internet, incredible advances in science and medicine—the list could go on endlessly. The assumption was that the human race would continue its evolution—always improving. However, modernism came crashing down with two world wars, genocide, ethnic cleans-ing, an AIDS epidemic, famine, and ultimately for North America with the fall of the Twin Towers on 9/11. The grand visions and metanarratives of modernism were shown to be illusions, and con-struction gave way to deconstruction. The small questioning voice of the postmodern minority is finally being heard above the din of modern super-powers.

Do you see how the values of Christian faith could fit into either one? It is possible that those of us raised in a modern cul-ture may identify Christianity with more things in the modern column—truth being absolute, for example—but an open spiritual

2. I'm thinking of Linkin Park's song "Somewhere to Belong" on their al-bum Meteora.

universe may actually be more conducive to authentic faith. This may be the experience of younger readers. Jesus and the early church were pre-modern, but consider them in the postmodern context. Jesus was heralded by a "voice crying in the wilderness," born in a stable to an unwed mother and a Jewish carpenter, and then became an itinerant local prophet and healer. Put in this way, Jesus seems quite at home in a postmodern culture. The communal nature of the early church as an alternative voice to the domineering empire that persecuted them also seems to connect with a postmodern culture.

There is another cultural shift happening simultaneously, and not unrelatedly, to the postmodern shift. This cultural shift is happening in church life and can be seen in the way that church relates to culture. Both of these shifts have a profound effect on spirituality and the way we live out our faith, but the shift from Christendom to post Christendom may be even more directly influential on our spirituality than the postmodern shift.

Christendom is the period of history tied to the Holy Roman Empire from the fourth to the sixteenth century but continuing on in a new western Christian nationalism characteristic of the seventeenth to the twentieth century, and perhaps continuing on today in a unique form in the USA. This Christendom has come to an end in Europe, with Canada, Australia, and finally, even the USA not far behind. Again, we must look at Christendom to understand post-Christendom.

During Christendom, the Christian church and its institutions were central and the Christian story was known by all in western civilization. Church buildings were in the center of towns and villages, with the steeple rising above all else. This was symbolic of the fact that Christians were the overwhelming majority in western society and "non-Christians" were urged to convert and, in some eras and places, even persecuted. In post-Christendom, the Christian story has been sidelined or forgotten completely: churches are seen as irrelevant relics on the fringes of society, and church buildings are often very literally museum pieces.

During Christendom, Christians enjoyed power and privilege and they felt at home in a society shaped by Christian values. In post-Christendom Christians are just one of many minority groups and, in fact, are now sometimes despised more than any other religious minority, primarily because of the history of Christendom. Christianity has been pushed to the margins. A lot of people have mourned the loss of privileges, the spurning of Christian values, biblical illiteracy, and the denigration of clergy. There are movements and cries to return to the good old days of Christendom; sermons and songs articulate the longing to "bring this nation back to God" and its apparent Christian foundations. Yet, perhaps post-Christendom is a blessing in disguise; perhaps it is an opportunity for the church to move from maintenance to mission, and from a moral majority to a witnessing minority. This may even be closer to the spirit of Jesus and the identity of the early church.

What do you think about these shifts? Should we embrace them or be wary? I feel particularly celebratory about the Christendom shift. It not only offers a new way to be church but a new way to be spiritual that may even allow us to better get at what Jesus had in mind when he called his first followers. How does the new spirituality look? Is it as varied as our postmodern clothing styles?

Post-Everything Spirituality

There are four themes that have characterized the spirituality of the first postmodern generation:

"Spiritual but not religious"

I am sure you have heard this line before. I do not need to quote a lot of statistics to back up the point that people are very interested in spirituality but not necessarily in going to churches, synagogues, mosques, or temples. Postmodern young people might be deeply suspicious of the institutional church, but they have popular respect for Jesus the nonconformist, or they may speak about a "personal relationship with Jesus." The first postmodern generation sees in the institutional church a static statement of faith, not a dynamic experience of the transcendent. They want to be part of something that moves them: a walk in the forest or listening to a good song can do just as well. So they turn to other communities that allow for a more personal experience, and they turn to a worship of celebrities, whether that is Jesus of Nazareth or Jennifer Lawrence.

On the other hand, Christian Smith, in an American study from 2009, reports that youth are remarkably conventional in their spiritual expression: just like their parents, they continue to be involved with religious institutions.[3] Youth are going to church, and church seems to make a difference in youth's lives. The one note of challenge in his research is that youth as a whole are not able to articulate their faith very well or explain how it makes a difference in their lives. The phrase "moral therapeutic deism" has been used to describe this new banal spirituality.[4] It is moral in the sense of living a good life, it is therapeutic in that faith helps one get through hard times, and it is deistic in that God is really not involved in every-day life. How do we explain these seemingly opposite trends?

Another saying might help us to get a handle on it: "Hardcore or not at all." Perhaps there is a hollowing-out of the religious middle ground in North America. Reginald Bibby, the University of Lethbridge sociologist who heads up Project Teen Canada, concludes that the grey zone of those who believe in God, but do not regularly practise an established religion, is rapidly emptying out, leaving behind two distinct camps: teens who are very religious and actively practise their religion, and those who do not believe in God at all.[5] There are a dizzying number of studies, often with contradictory results. Perhaps this is itself an indication that postmodern spirituality is like a mosaic, and not at all monolithic.

3. Smith, *Souls in Transition*.
4. Dean, "How to Avoid Raising Nice Teenagers."
5. Bibby, *The Emerging Millennials*, 180–186.

"Experience is Sacred"

"Truth happens. Truth is an event to be experienced, not merely believed [and as a result,] every form of intense personal experience from orgasm to roller coasters is potentially 'spiritual' for young people."[6] Postmodern youth have a profound hunger for immediate experience. They are more inclined to rely on personal experience than on the accounts of others. Truth through self-discovery is seen as superior to that handed down by creed or custom. Immediate experience is sensual. Postmodern spirituality is an embodied spirituality, and thus the body itself is a source of religious meaning for one's life;[7] the body is not only physical, it is also spiritual. The growing popularity of body piercing and tattooing is an example of this obsession with the body as an expression of spirituality. Many such bodily markings are very religious in nature. Ask people about their tattoo and you will often get a personal testimony of spirituality.

As the body is spiritual, so then is sexuality. Sex and God are closely related.[8] "They [postmodern young people] know that they are at once both body and soul, that they desire both sex and spirit, and that the object of their desire lies both beyond them and within them."[9] Kenda Creasy Dean continues by pointing out that even in the Bible and medieval Christian mysticism, erotic experience is a helpful tool for learning about God. Desire is desire and the direction or object of our desire is what determines moral character.[10] The sacredness of the body and sexuality is all about a relational spirituality. Relationships embody fidelity and convey truth; they are opportunities to invest our lives in something or someone. To be true is not to be factual but to be loyal.[11]

6. Dean, "X-Files," 12.
7. Beaudoin, *Virtual Faith*, 77.
8. Bell, *SexGod*.
9. Dean, "Holding On to Our Kisses," 10.
10. Ibid., 11.
11. Dean, "X Files," 10.

"Sensitivity to Suffering"

Sometimes we think that no generation of youth has had it as good as the present one, with money and choices galore. However, "When a generation bears the weight of so many failures—including AIDS, divorce, abuse, poor schools, recessions, youth poverty, teen suicide, failure of governmental and religious institutions, national debt, high taxes, environmental devastation, drugs, parents that need to be parented, violence, unstable economic security, premature loss of childhood—how can suffering not be an important part of one's identity?"[12]

The "war on terrorism" in Iraq and Afghanistan has shaped the spirituality of a generation, not only of young soldiers returning—if they are fortunate—from the battlefield, but of those who are watching the reality on television and experiencing not only the pain of the people on the other side of the globe, but that of their own dysfunctional families and violent communities at home. This is why the cross—a tool of capital punishment and symbol of suffering—has almost instant credibility for postmodern people. Even those who do not worship Jesus as the Son of God wear crosses.

The postmodern generation is also marked by realism, being the first generation that does not expect to exceed their parents' financial position—and often do not want to. They seem to intuitively know how to live with both existential hardship and material want.

"Blue Like Jazz"

Donald Miller's book, *Blue Like Jazz*, captures the spirituality of postmodern Christianity.[13] Jazz music has a basic structure around which musicians play off of each other and improvise, according to their skills, as their emotions and the music move them. Postmodern spirituality is all about improvisation, tinkering, and bricolage, as numerous observers and writers have noted.[14] As young people

12. Beaudoin, *Virtual Faith*, 104.

13. Miller, *Blue Like Jazz*.

14. Burke and Taylor, *A Heretic's Guide*, chapter 6; Wuthnow, *After the Baby Boomers*, chapter 6.

experience life they improvise their spirituality on the go. It is like a series of vignettes rather than a logical narrative—as illustrated by the now cult-classic film, *Napoleon Dynamite*. This might help us to make sense of the confusing trends we examined initially.

There are a number of practices that display this spirituality of improvisation. One of these is experimenting with different beliefs from different traditions or even religions. An entertaining but poignant caricature of this is seen in the main protagonist of the novel (and recent film adaptation), *Life of Pi*, who converts to every religion—just to cover all the bases. This generation is also known for church shopping and hopping, or participating in more than one at a time—and generally not committing themselves to any particular denomination or tradition. They have an open theology and see God as mystery, not as captured in a particular dogma or theological framework. It is not spirituality without religion; rather, it is spirituality first and then religion, as it is suitable and pliable for improvisation.

Another practice that complements this fluidity is the openness to questions, even to the point of labelling the questioning itself as a sacred activity.[15] Postmodern spirituality embraces ambiguity and is content to live with unanswered questions. The ultimate spiritual question for the postmodern generation is not, "Can I believe this is true?" but "Will you be there for me?"[16] This displays not only improvisation but the importance of experience and relationships.

15. Dark, *The Sacredness of Questioning Everything*.
16. Beaudoin, *Virtual Faith*, 140.

For Reflection

What evidence have you seen of the cultural shifts mentioned? Are these shifts helpful or harmful for the church and Christian spirituality? How? Why?

Which one of the postmodern spiritual themes has been most prevalent in your experience and observation? How?

How has your spirituality been shaped by this major cultural shift in our society? How do you feel about this?

10

Logo Wear: Economic Spirituality in a Culture of Consumerism

CALVIN AND HOBBES HAS always been one of my favorite comic strips—there is a great deal of wisdom to be found in the young rascal and his stuffed tiger. A favorite strip is the one where Calvin is despairingly looking down at his plain striped shirt and saying, "I wish my shirt had a logo or a product on it." Hobbes is obviously confused as Calvin continues: "A good shirt turns the wearer into a walking corporate billboard! It says to the world, 'My identity is so wrapped up in what I buy that I paid the company to advertise its products!'" Hobbes replies, "You admit to that?" Calvin responds pragmatically and proudly, "Oh sure, endorsing products is the American way to express individuality." And it is true. It is difficult to find a piece of clothing without a logo on it—we are all walking advertisements! Often, the clothing without a brand name or visible logo is seen as suspect or of poor quality.

What we buy is who we are. In all of the other chapters I was using clothing as an analogy—in this chapter it is more than an analogy, it is an example. This chapter, like the last one but unlike some of the others, is also very present rather than historical. Sometimes, it is easier to critically examine clothing we have worn in the past than what we have on now.

LOGO WEAR

The Power of Branding

Corporate branding influences how we see ourselves today. This is troubling but I believe it is true. "Whether we see it or not, whether young people go along or rebel against them, brands strongly influence teen and young adult self-understanding."[1] This is only true for the present—brands did not influence previous generations in the same way—but that does not mean it has not affected older people as well (we just choose different brands to associate ourselves with).

The forces of globalization are also at work. There is an accelerated interconnectedness and interdependence of individuals and cultures of the world. Due to ease of travel and communication, there is more of a global consciousness in the world. As a result, brands transcend national and continental boundaries. Coca-Cola's jingle, "I'd like to buy the world a coke" is a good early example of this. Coke has gone on to become the world's most popular drink. Its logo can be found on every continent and in every socio-economic neighborhood—even in refugee camps!

By focusing on branding, companies definitely hope to make money, but deeper than that, they hope to make their logos into a personality. Each brand has a lifestyle, an image, an identity, or a set of values attached to it. What kind of brands do you associate with? What drinks are in your fridge? What kind of snacks are on your coffee table? What kind of vehicle is out in your parking stall? What kind of clothing hangs in your closet? Consider what kind of personality is associated with each of these brands you find around your home. Although there is no one set of brands for everyone, each one represents a particular identity.

There is spiritual power in these branded objects. No object transmits spiritual power in and of itself, but we invest it with meaning both individually and socially. Does Jesus have a logo? Are economic concerns important to Christian spirituality? How, and how deeply, do I integrate who I am in faith with what I buy? Is there such as thing as an economic spirituality? How is Jesus God's economist?

1. Beaudoin, *Consuming Faith,* 3.

As brands conjure up identities for people, they draw attention away from the products themselves and how they were produced. This is called corporate dualism. To stay competitive, global corporations try to distance themselves from earthbound issues like workers, wages, and factories, and the practice of contracting out has become more and more common. Logos no longer have anything to do with the products or production but with a certain ethos that floats above and apart from them. Corporations advertise the brand as an ideal experience or lifestyle, separate from the commodity and its earthly, bodily associations; that is, the who, when, where, how, and why of its production. Yet, it is real, bodily people who sweat and bleed, who give these brands material life. For many large corporations these bodies are merely a necessary evil dealt with minimally and at a distance.[2]

Christians are also widely perceived to be spirit/body dualists, secretive about sexuality, skeptical about the spiritual value of physical pleasure, afraid of the flesh and carnality. Paul addressed this in many of his letters now contained in the New Testament.[3] Docetism, the early gnostic heresy that Jesus could not have had a real human body, is alive and well today. We may not conceptually deny the bodily humanity of Jesus, but we do in the way we live. We deny Jesus' humanity when we deny the holiness of our own bodies and the pleasure of bodily activities such as eating, playing, and making love. Many assert that they believe in Jesus but conduct their economic relationships according to strictly so-called secular market criteria. This is practical Docetism and dualism of body and soul.

We become like Jesus, not by denying our bodiliness but by embracing it. Being a body is part of being human: we are bodies; we do not merely have a body. The incarnation is one of the most radical teachings in any religion, and Jesus talks more about money and possessions than about prayer, worship, and evangelism put together! Yet, the latter are the topics and activities that

2. See section 3 in the video, *The Corporation*, for further insights on this idea.

3. 1 Timothy 4 is a good example.

often consume our energy and time. In order to live incarnation-
ally we must develop an economic spirituality. Let us hear it from
Jesus himself, as put into contemporary English by John Henson:

> Someone in the crowd shouted out to Jesus, "Teacher, my
> brother's done me out of my share of the family property.
> Tell him to put it right." Jesus said, "I'm not a judge. I'm
> not qualified to judge your case. But I will say this, to
> you and everybody else: Watch that monster 'Greed.'
> Quality of life doesn't depend on how much money or
> property you have.
>
> Then Jesus told a story. "There was once a rich farm-
> er whose farm over-produced. He was short of storage
> space he needed while waiting for the prices to be right.
> It caused him great anxiety. 'What am I going to do?' he
> thought to himself. Then he made a big decision. 'I know,'
> he said, 'I'll pull down these old barns and build bigger
> and better ones. Then with room for surplus, I'll be able
> to retire on the profits. I'll be able to do all the things
> I've always wanted to do, take holidays abroad, go to par-
> ties and have a good time.' But God said, 'you chump!
> This is the last day of your life. Your wealth is useless to
> you now. You're so thoughtless, you haven't even made
> a will!' That's what people are like who spend their time
> making money and don't give God a chance to give them
> things of real value."
>
> Jesus turned to his friends and said, "Stop worrying
> about things of no importance. What does it matter what
> you eat or drink or whether your clothes are in fashion?
> A good life doesn't depend on going to posh restaurants
> or having the right wardrobe. Take a tip from the crows.
> They don't go to work every day, or put their money in
> a bank when they get paid, but God makes sure they
> have something to eat. You rate yourselves more highly
> than the birds, don't you? You won't make your life last
> any longer by worrying about it. What's the point of
> worry when there's so little you can do to change things?
> Be like the wild flowers. They don't earn their living, yet
> they're better dressed than Solomon with all his beads and
> bangles! Since God cares so much about the looks of the
> grass which ends up as stubble in a matter of days, God is

bound to see to your clothes. It's more trust you need! It's time to stop vexing yourselves with questions like, 'Where shall we eat tonight?' or 'Have we ordered the right wine to go with the meal?' You'll make yourselves ill, having to make so many decisions! People who are bothered by such questions don't yet know God. God loves you, and knows what's best for you. Help to bring about God's New World. Then there'll be enough for everybody.

Don't be frightened if the tasks ahead seem too big for so few of you. The New World is God's project. The Loving God will make a present of it to you. So sell all those luxuries and give the money to charity. Treasure those things that last the test of time. That way you won't need to worry about burglars or breaking things. You can tell what a person is like by what they value.[4]

Developing an Economic Spirituality

The first task in developing a Christian economic spirituality is to accept the mysterious spiritual depth of human identity.[5] Who am I if I accept that I am what I possess? Identity has a lot to do with where I spend most of my money. We know in our heads that Christian identity is to be rooted in God, not in Mammon—which is an alternative god—but which of these gives us our primary identity? The first step towards discovery is to begin to contemplate the depths of our identity in God and also to model and teach that to our children. We are the beloved children of God.

A second task is to cultivate a spiritual indifference to numbers. Too often in our culture, divine blessing is equated with personal wealth, good attendance at church events, or the media attention generated by our social justice campaigns. At youth pastor gatherings we often compared numbers: How many kids are in your youth group? How many kids are from unchurched homes? The bigger the numbers were, the better your youth ministry in

4. Luke 12:13–34. Henson, *Good as New,* 210–211.

5. This section on developing an economic spirituality is based on Beaudoin, *Consuming Faith,* chapter 6.

the eyes of God and peers (or so we thought). Yet God and the things of God cannot be commoditized. At a recent walk for an important cause, the numbers reported to the media were vastly inflated in order to make it appear successful. The church in North America has been infiltrated practically by the prosperity gospel, even if not always doctrinally.[6]

Visual media is particularly prone to experiences of disembodiment; thus, we should be wary of our consumption of visual media. With visual media we can watch the world without getting involved in it. In a visual culture, it is easy to see humans as disembodied people. The people on the screen or on the page become less than human—the characters are more real than the actual people who play their parts. When our children were small we encouraged them to talk back to the screen; a practice that hopefully helped them to be aware of real human issues in advertising, or in the shows themselves. The spiritual practice of hospitality and community with food and drink are great antidotes to these problems of disembodiment.

Besides the obvious—that is, preaching and teaching the many economic texts in the Gospels—how can the church participate in developing an economic spirituality? It is important to cultivate a balance between the active and contemplative life, between doing acts of service, and just being in the presence of God. The church as patron of the arts can also be a way of cultivating an embodied spirituality. Art symbolizes an embodied, incarnational spirituality. God fashioned people out of clay and yet we are called the image of God. The stuff of art—pigment, paper, clay, wire, ivory, wood, metal, flesh—combined with human breath and muscle becomes deeply spiritual and God-like.

Finally, Skye Jethani, in his book, *The Divine Commodity*, urges the practicing of the classic spiritual disciplines as radical nonconformity to the religion of Consumerism.[7] Instead of the commodification of God, we practice the simple faith and imagination of a child. Instead of the noise and commotion of buying

6. See the concluding chapter in Bowler, *Blessed*.
7. Jethani, *The Divine Commodity*.

and selling experiences in stores and in worship services, we practice silence and contemplative prayer. Instead of the giving in to the media's manufacturing of desire and its ideology of scarcity,[8] we practice simplicity and fasting. Instead of the individualization and homogeneity provided by endless consumer choice, we practice diversity in community. Instead of the dehumanization of suburban privacy fences, private electronic devices, and fear of the other, we practice hospitality and welcome.

And, of course, careful discernment about our personal and communal economic decisions is the direct approach to an economic spirituality. We are managers, or stewards, of all the gifts and all of creation that God has entrusted to us. By acting in solidarity with creators and producers of products we are combatting dualism and practicing an economic spirituality. In North America we have the luxury of choice about what to buy and consume, and where we invest. This luxury also comes with a responsibility.

Perhaps boycotting our local malls is too easy, but it is one small symbolic thing I do to practice an economic spirituality. In the spirit of Reverend Billy and the Church of Stop Shopping,[9] I offer a humorous satirical piece I wrote many years ago to close this chapter.

The Mall Conspiracy

There is a building that wants to take over my community and the world! That building is the Seven Oaks Mall—or if you have mall envy pick any mall near you, it will do just as well. I believe that this building is the so-called "abomination of desolation" referred to in the Old Testament book of Daniel (9:27, 11:31, 12:11) and then quoted by Jesus in the New Testament. In the past people have speculated about the identity of the abomination: Was it Roman conquerors in the temple in 70 CE? Is it the Islamic mosque built on the holy hill in Jerusalem? Is it the graven image that

---

8. This concept is elucidated in chapter 4 of Cavanaugh, *Being Consumed*.

9. See www.revbilly.com.

the Anti-Christ will set up in the temple in Jerusalem during the last days? End your speculation! I have found the identity of the abomination of desolation: it is the mall.

I have always had this eerie chill go up my spine whenever I drive by the mall and see the bright, colorful signs, hundreds of cars in the parking lot, and people streaming in like there is no tomorrow. It is like there is something evil and sinister going on inside this sprawling building; like they are going inside to worship at some forbidden altar; like they might not ever come out alive. The mall is a house of false material worship.

I actually had to go inside the mall once, when my son won a prize in the Science Fair and they made him display his project in the mall of all places! The irony is that his project was on the environmental effects of constructing roads and buildings. I was sure it was some kind of sinister plot to try and get unsuspecting parents like myself into the "abomination" just so they could steal our money! I dashed in just long enough to see him collect his prize from the naturalist society, all the while hearing evil voices inside my head, "shop, shop, shop, you'll feel much better when you shop, shop, shop." I tried not to look around—just being there made me shudder with revulsion.

Good theology should not be based on mere feelings and personal experiences. It should come from solid empirical and biblical research. People might scoff and say, "This is only your personal experience. I've had many trips to the mall and the people inside are perfectly normal and they are selling perfectly legitimate wares in perfectly legitimate ways." Hear me out—it may save your life.

All biblical terms must be interpreted in their proper context and so also the identification of the "abomination of desolation" must come from interpreting the term in its proper context. From the context in Daniel it is clear that the "abomination that causes desolation" refers to a building that sets itself up as an alternative worship space to the temple, the dwelling place of God. Is this is not exactly what the mall does? It is now open on Sunday. It is the place where people go to pay their ultimate allegiance—drop most of their money—and it is there that they fellowship with like-minded believers in the food court.

The term itself also holds a key to its identification. An "abomination" is something that is "disgusting, intensely hated, or loathed" or an "ill omen," according to Webster's Dictionary. The outward appearance of a mall does not seem so bad, but the Evil One lurks around every corner store in the mall seducing innocent people into making life-destroying purchases. Once a person goes inside it gets a hold on you and you are involuntarily drawn into its evil clutches, compelled to return again and again even though you hate yourself for all the money you leave there when all you get in return is an empty feeling.

"Desolation" is the action of leaving something in ruins, as in a barren wasteland. This is exactly what a mall does to the environment, to your pocketbook, and to your soul. Earth, grass, flowers, and trees are ruined by concrete and pavement; your wallet is left barren and empty, and your soul is left the same.

It all fits! It all makes sense! Why have we not seen this before? People all over North America rushing headlong to the mall only to be devoured and consumed by this arch enemy of The Most High.

A building such as this is none other than the abomination of desolation: more dangerous than a despot, more luring than a brothel, more captivating than a cult! Buyers beware.

Unfortunately, this is not just clever satire. On Friday, November 28, 2008 Jdimytai Damour, a temporary worker at a Wal-Mart store in Valley Stream, New York was trampled to death as two thousand bargain hunters surged through the store's doors at five in the morning. Jdimytai's death is a curse on all of us. Consumerism has become the dominant religion in North America. We kill and we die for its god. As followers of Jesus we must take responsibility for our part in what our culture has become. Let us cease our hand wringing and holier-than-thou finger pointing and begin to cultivate an economic spirituality.

For Reflection:

How has your spirituality been influenced by the religion of consumerism? Why is it so difficult to see in ourselves?

What are some small and practical ways for you to begin living an economic spirituality?

11

Torn Jeans: Facing Our
Own Woundedness

IN MY PARENTS' GENERATION, torn clothing was an embarrass-
ment and a sign of poverty and patches were sown on as quickly as
possible. No longer! Now, companies pre-tear jeans to give them a
worn out look. Perhaps it has something to do with "sensitivity to
suffering" as a characteristic of postmodern spirituality. Generally
though, when clothes are torn or stained, they are damaged goods
and most people prefer not to wear them. Clothes are thrown out
if the tear is too great or if the stain is too deep because patching
clothes and darning socks has become a lost art.

By now you know where the analogy is going: stains and
tears are disruptive, damaging, marking—painful. A patch is like
a scar on our skin: a constant reminder of a wound. We can throw
out our damaged clothes and buy new ones so we do not have to
think about the stain or tear anymore, but we cannot do that in life.
Just as stains and tears in our clothing are a normal part of wearing clothes, so also are wounds a normal part of life. "Everybody
hurts," as the band REM sang a number of years ago. All people
experience pain and loss—it is a universal part of human experience—and even though these experiences may be very different
externally (loss of a job or dwelling, death of a loved one, separation or divorce, betrayal or abuse by an authority, ruin of reputa-
tion or relationship, retirement, accident, illness . . . the list goes
on), there may be some profound similarities internally. We have

all been wounded in some way, and perhaps the deepest wounds are internal—on our souls, our identities.

Although we should not wish pain on anyone including ourselves, it has been my—and many others'—experience that wounds can become an integral part of our spiritual formation. As with all our spiritual clothing, we may as well confess; in this case, to the fact that we have some stains on our shirts and tears in our jeans. The sooner we do the sooner we can move on to healing and health. These wounds can only become part of who we are, part of our spiritual formation, as we acknowledge the wound, examine and reflect on it, and allow the Great Physician to perform the necessary surgeries.

My Story of Woundedness and Healing

I was a veteran youth pastor, sitting at a youth worker's retreat listening to the speaker talking about how to understand and counsel youth who had been victims of sexual abuse, when something began to awaken inside me. I awoke to the nightmarish reality that I was the abused kid he was talking about.

That retreat is now more than two decades in the past, but it was the beginning of a long and difficult journey of healing from childhood sexual abuse that has become a significant part of my personal spiritual formation and my ministry to youth and young adults.

Kids who are abused, sexually or otherwise, have lost their childhood innocence. They have been robbed of it and have been left instead with a bag of scars and memories that they are unable to deal with. There are numerous self-protective defense mechanisms that victims like myself use in order to survive the trauma of abuse; for example, an abused child is not able to feel the full emotions of pain, fear or rage that are associated with abuse. If they could, they would go crazy. What often happens, therefore, is that the terrible memories and accompanying emotions are blocked or repressed involuntarily until adulthood. Along with repression, there might also be denial or rationalization of the experiences. "It happened so long ago." "Worse things have happened to others." "Maybe it was all just a bad dream." "He really didn't mean anything by it."

Survivors of childhood abuse sometimes become excellent people helpers themselves. In a strange sort of way, helping other people to deal with their pain becomes a way to avoid facing one's own. This is who I was. I became a caring and outgoing youth pastor. As I look back, there seems to be certain types of young people who were drawn to my ministry and to whom I was drawn to pay attention to. A number of these kids had been victims of abuse themselves. I believe that they may have been attracted to my ministry, unconsciously knowing that they would receive the empathetic response of a fellow traveler.

I had, and continue to have, a deep desire to help young people who have been victims of abuse, who struggle with low self-esteem, who find it hard to assert themselves in relationships or tasks. But at that retreat, I began to realize that I was the abused kid with low self-esteem who needed the ministry of healing.

A few years after the retreat, I went to a spiritual director to get help for the spiritual stream that had run dry within me. I was expecting some accountability for my spiritual disciplines or some advice on how to pray better. Instead, I was led to the mirror of my soul to look at myself and the wounds of my past. The trickle of living water on my spiritual streambed did not come as I expected. Although I would not wish any kind of trauma on any person, it has been through my wounds that God has shaped me for life and ministry. That is one of the mysteries of divine work.

I have regained my childhood innocence: the lost boy has been found. I was born again, a grown man, free and empowered to be who I was created to be. In a strange kind of way, God used the most terrible thing in my life to bring me new insight, joy, and meaning.[1]

---

1. Renée Altson's courage in sharing her journey of healing in *Stumbling Toward Faith* has given me courage to share mine.

The Stations on the Journey of Healing

Emotional and spiritual healing is like physical healing in many ways. The deeper the hurt the longer it takes to heal. Healing happens from the inside out so it is helpful not to close up the wound too fast. I found this out very graphically when my appendix burst and I had an open wound for almost a week as the poison drained out of my system. Just as untreated wounds fester and can become infected and need to be lanced, so also can emotional wounds turn into bitterness and illness and need to be dealt with deeply and honestly. Scars and scabs are a sign of healing: they remind us of how we have been healed and offer hope to other sufferers. We should not rush the healing process even though it is human nature to do away with pain as fast as possible. Ultimately, all healing involves cooperation between the patient and the doctor. Although surgery is performed by a doctor while the patient is asleep, in all other aspects the one with the wound or disease is involved in the process in some way. Spiritual healing is ultimately the work of God, but as we discovered earlier, we are co-laborers in our own spiritual formation.

One of the most important things to understand is that healing is most often a journey, not an event. For some the journey may take a few months, and for others many years, even for the same wound. Time is a great healer. There is no single prescribed journey of healing, but there are some common stations along the way. The stages of healing may happen in a different order, with varying intensity, and some of us may not experience certain stages at all. Sometimes, people will experience the stages simultaneously and even repeatedly, like the peeling of an onion or as if traveling in a circle. Although the phases of healing will follow my own journey, and include poems specific to my experience, I believe the journey of healing is similar for all kinds of wounds.

Denial

The first stop on the journey is often one of denial or minimization of the wound. "It was not that bad; worse things have happened to others." Sometimes, it is like shock: we are not able to deal with the trauma and so the memories are blocked until we are able to face it. I was not fully conscious of my abuse until twenty years after the fact when the memories came roaring back. Other times, denial is a defense mechanism that works like an anesthetic. The infamous Winnipeg winter illustrates this stage for me; it became the season of my soul that I could not break out of for many years.

Winter

It is so frigid,
and day after day
it is
for so long,
that even
the fastest flowing river
has iced up
rigid.

With every hint of winterbourne
another cold
SNAP!
Everything is frozen in
this arctic burial ground;
stuck,
immovable.
I can't even break out
to fly south.

Fear

When circumstances or counseling melt the numbness of denial or minimization, the emotions often come back like a flood, commonly beginning with fear and paranoia. These may include fears of death, change, or simply the fear of the unknown. For me, some of the fear manifested itself in irrational behaviors. I could not answer the phone for fear that it would be my abuser. What we are unable to bear or understand in our conscious life often comes out in the unconscious and so I experienced night terrors and nightmares such as I had never had before. While this appeared to be a dream about my young son, it was really about me.

Powerlessness

Huge and yellow
block black letters
that say "Caterpillar"
it's a bulldozer
moving the earth
shaping exterior reality
impressively
making roads and ditches
with rumbling noise
and persistent movement
in all kinds of terrain

nearing a cliff
over the edge
it falls fast and hard
smashing, crashing
upside down
squished underneath
a boy driver
out of control
helpless
and needing
911

Pain

Of course, a wound hurts—it is painful—and when something hurts, we cry. Those who have been wounded often experience deep inner pain and a sense of loss. The loss may be innocence, it may be a loved one, it may be a sense of safety, it may be a relationship, it may be a job, and it may be many other things. This phase of healing involves deep grief and mourning of that loss. The beauty of the Christian Gospel is that healing comes through the one who was wounded for us.[2] Although I do not pretend to have any understanding of what Jesus went through in Gethsemane or on the cross, I also cried out for companionship and empathy in the midst of my pain.

My Dearest Friend

Please wait with me one hour
my dearest friend;
the dark of night is now at hand.
I bear the burden, wound
of someone else's sin
and to the skies I cry,
"Please take away from me
this cup of sorrow, suffering."
Must I bear it all alone?

Wait with me one hour
my dearest friend
in this dark night of my soul.
Oh that I could sweat great drops of blood
or cry with seas of tears
or scream and roar,
a frightened cornered beast,
but I wait in silent anguish,
plunged the knife,

2. 1 Peter 2:24.

my soul lies bleeding.
Can I bear to feel the pain?

"If it be Thy will
I will."
But wait with me
this hour my
dearest friend.

Despair

The energy that is required to deal with fear and pain generally leaves one exhausted and despairing. Bouts of depression and feelings of hopelessness are not uncommon in this stage of the healing journey. A frequent phrase in the psalms of lament is, "How long?" "How long will this pain last? I don't think I can take it any longer." There is a sense of having nothing left with which to continue the journey of healing. Death seems like the easiest way out. This is when it is common for people to contemplate suicide or have death wishes.

Death Wish

on the edge of tears
past the plain of melancholy
forced there by pain
teetering precariously
afraid of what lies below
yet wanting to fall
let go
die

Anger

Ironically, the most energizing emotion is also the one that is sometimes spurned by those on a healing journey. Yet, it is right for us to be angry with injustice, suffering, brokenness, and loss. Anger brings energy, strength, and action to these situations. Anger finally helps us to become active in dealing with our wound. Anger can also be harmful and dangerous to oneself and to others, though, so it must be managed carefully. I had a hard time getting angry with my abuser, and found it was easier to make excuses for him. To help me, my spiritual director gave me some visualization exercises and rituals to perform. A number of biblical stories became very personal and autobiographical for me.[3]

Lazarus

I am dead
killed by the powers that oppress
bound by the sins of the fathers
embalmed in the stench of abuse
entombed in the grip of the evil one
decaying with hopelessness and fear

I am dead
four days
But wait (oh I wait
in my death) it is the Master's voice I hear
enraged with passion
LOUD
He calls my name
"Live! Come out!"

I struggle against the death clothes

3. She had me visualize Jesus coming upon the scene of my childhood abuse and responding as he did with the cleansing of the temple in Matthew 21:12–16. In this case my body was the temple that was being cleansed.

bound so tight around me
stumbling towards the light
"Unbind him!" he commands to death
"Let him go free!"

I am alive.

Healing

The final stop on the journey of healing is acceptance, forgiveness, healing, and sometimes the reconciliation of relationships. This is divine work and the domain of the Holy Spirit. It is God who heals, forgives, and reconciles. Acceptance, forgiveness, and healing can happen internally, but reconciliation needs the cooperation of others. It may be desirable but it is not always possible, and it is not essential for personal healing to take place. Healing, too, has various levels of depth. There may be a dramatic moment of realization, or it may come very gradually and almost imperceptibly. For me, it was a sense of coming home to a restored innocence and a new identity. It also involved a meeting with the perpetrator where he expressed his remorse and I was able to express a word of forgiveness. This significant layer of my healing corresponded to a geographical and denominational change at the time, and the reclaiming of my childhood name which I had abandoned for a few decades.

Home

My heart is home.
Your freshly fallen snow
has covered the brown and gray
and much dirt
that has been cursing
through my veins
and twisting body,
past.

Present:
peaceful, pure
Your home is safe,
I can call it mine.
I'll rest a while
even though I journey
I'll always be home
with you.

The Ongoing Journey

By facing our own traumas, shadows, shortcomings, hurts, and wounds—whatever they are; by being honest with God and ourselves about who we are, we create opportunities for others to be real with themselves and to come to us for healing ministry. This is a very difficult thing to do as it was for me. But until we do this, we will continue to be—often unconsciously—too preoccupied with ourselves to really listen to other people in pain. Jesus' example of the wounded healer has become the basis for my ongoing ministry with college students. I am both the wounded minister and the healing minister at the same time. I cannot separate one from the other.[4]

How does this look in daily life or ministry? It does not mean that we hang out all of our dirty laundry, so to speak, every time we talk to people, or that we shock them with the sordid details of our past experiences. It does mean that we are conscious of the fact that we live and minister out of our own woundedness. It does mean that we are honest about our own wounds with those we relate to so that we can be truly with them in their unique experiences. Each time I share of myself with my wounds I am vulnerable. I take the risk of misunderstanding or rejection, and relive the pain to some extent—just as it is happening to me as I write—but each experience also brings a measure of healing personally and opens the door of invitation for others to entrust their wounded selves to the Wounded Healer whom I represent as a minister.

4. Henri Nouwen's *Wounded Healer* has become my manual for ministry in this regard.

For Reflection

What wounds have been part of your life experience?

What stations of the healing journey have you experienced? Which ones need some deeper work and more time?

How have your wounds and the journey of healing contributed to your spiritual formation?

12

Get Dressed! Putting on the Christian Clothes

WHAT KIND OF CLOTHES are you wearing as you read this? Does it matter what kind of clothes we wear? What kind of clothing should Christ's followers wear? As a teenager, I remember having arguments with my parents about what kind of clothes I put on for the Sunday morning worship service. We had "Sunday clothes" and "every-day clothes" and there was no mixing the two because wearing nice clothes to go to church was a way to show respect for God. The idea was that since religious activities were of utmost importance, special attire was required. I guess we have relaxed somewhat, because today we are just happy our teens are in church regardless what they wear! Yet the metaphorical question remains: What kind of clothes do Christians wear?

I have used the analogy of clothing throughout the book. In each chapter we have noted some items of clothing that have shaped who we have become. In this chapter, I want to look ahead to some ideals and explore the clothes of Christian maturity. Ephesians 4:13 says that the goal is to "reach unity in the faith and in the knowledge of the Son of God and become mature, attaining to the whole measure of the fullness of Christ." What does this look like? Are there some qualities of character that we should all strive to exhibit? What qualities does a spiritually formed person display? What kind of clothes are they wearing?

Numerous authors, churches, and task forces have sought to delineate what Christian maturity looks like.[1] James Fowler summarizes Daniel Jenkins' earlier work using Paul and the Sermon on the Mount. Together, they say that Christian maturity consists of the following qualities:[2]

1. Meekness, meaning a gentle strength controlled by a love for God and a desire for righteousness.

2. Being a peacemaker by tending to the health of relationships and community.

3. Generosity, meaning the qualities of spending and being spent for the other out of gratitude.

4. Magnanimity, meaning largeness of spirit or the ability to focus on what is most important.

5. Joyfulness, not primarily referring to the emotion, but rather to the ability to be genuinely festive in the midst of a world of suffering.

Although it is an interesting exercise to compare all the different definitions and descriptions of Christian maturity developed by various theological traditions, the Christian Scriptures also give us some succinct and profound lists of character qualities.[3] There is even one that fits our clothing analogy, dare I say it, like a glove! Colossians 3:12–17 talks about the clothes the people of Christ are to be dressed up in. Although it uses the metaphor of getting dressed, the clothes are inward qualities. Let the following meditation on these qualities serve as a concluding garment of exhortation to all the other clothes we have accumulated throughout our lives. Each quality will also have a suggested practice, spiritual

---

1. A few of my favorite descriptions of Christian faith maturity are found in: Smith, *Called to Be Saints*; Augsburger, *Dissident Discipleship*; Roehlkepartain and Griggs, *The Teaching Church*. Another extensive description, developed by the Mennonite Brethren denomination, can be found at: http://www.mb-conf.ca/home/products_and_services/resources/tools_for_the_local_church/description_of_a_growing_disciple/

2. Fowler, *Becoming Adult*, 101–102.

3. 1 Peter 2:3–11; Galatians 5:22; Matthew 5:3–12.

discipline, or ritual to help us put on this item of clothing in daily life. Before we get to the qualities, we put them in the context of the book of Colossians.

"Therefore"

The "therefore" here ties this text to the Christocentric theme of the entire book, and most directly to the previous verses, 3:1–11. There, the negative qualities are listed: these are the clothes that Christ's followers should take off. Verse 11 concludes that, in Christ, ethnicity, socio-economic status, gender, or any other human difference, is not what defines our relationships. We are all one in Christ Jesus, therefore:

"As God's chosen people holy and dearly loved"

Paul offers readers a vision of an alternative community in contrast with the powers and principalities that Christ has defeated. The book of Colossians argues for the uniqueness of Christ. Claims for Christian uniqueness are quite common, but they are often made with arrogance or even violence—which is completely contradictory to the way of Christ. In Colossians 1 Paul describes how everything was created through Christ and how everything will be redeemed by Christ. Christ is the head of the church and the church is to be a witness to this reconciliation of all things. In a sense, life in the church is to be an example of what all of life is to be like—a scary thought when we look at the reality in our churches! Perhaps part of our problem is that we forget how deeply we are loved. The foundation of our identity in Christ is that we are beloved daughters and sons of God.[4] We are loved before we have a chance to put any clothes on! The beginning of spiritual formation is "Jesus loves me, this I know."

What does this alternative community look like? What kind of clothes are the people wearing? The clothes are what are visible

4. See Nouwen, *Life of the Beloved.*

to others. These are inner qualities, yet are on display for the rest of the world. We witness by the clothes we wear, and I am not talking about T-shirts with Christian slogans on them! All the qualities are about how we live together and treat one another, not so much about private inner piety but about corporate life. They are the communal clothes of the Christian community.

"Clothe yourselves with:"

"Compassion"

The King James Version translates this as, "bowels of mercy." In those days bowels were considered the innermost depths of a human being. In other words, compassion comes from the depths of a person and empathizes and reaches out to others. Compassion is a shared passion; thus, a person of compassion has deep feelings for other people, especially those who are hurting or are experiencing broken relationships. A compassionate church is a welcoming church whose heart goes out to those who are suffering or marginalized. Archbishop William Temple once said that "the church is the only institution that exists for the sake of its non-members." It reaches out in compassion in a deep and genuine way.

Find a picture of a person you care about deeply who is hurting presently. It could be a person in your family or a picture from a newspaper of a person whom you do not even know personally. Carry this picture with you for a day to remind you to pray for this person.

"Kindness"

Kindness comes from the same English root as kin signifying that all people are to be treated as family. Kindness is like denim: practical. "In contrast to the cold-hearted bottom line of profit margins and market shares, Paul envisions a community that places something as inefficient and unprofitable as kindness at its heart."[5] After all, the church is a non-profit organization! "Kindness is a listening, caring presence in the midst of a world that rushes by and often doesn't see people or their needs."[6]

It is as simple as opening the door for someone or letting someone else have the parking stall you were eyeing on a busy shopping day. The idea to do random acts of kindness for complete strangers, or even family and friends, is a wonderful trend. Why not make it deliberate and intentional rather than merely random and spontaneous?

"Humility"

If we look at history, the church has not always been a humble institution. We have proudly stated, "Our head is the Savior of the world and the Lord of the Universe and we have creeds and councils to prove it. If only people would believe in Jesus like we do the world's problems would be solved." This attitude is not the humble clothing that the writer of Colossians is talking about. Humility is not about having all the answers but about co-struggling with the questions. It is not about dressing in rags but about seeing ourselves rightly, the bad and the good. Our humility is to be in contrast to the arrogant pride of the empire that refuses to admit a mistake.

Humility is a difficult quality to make tangible. Jesus' act of washing his disciples' feet is a good example; where he did something that was always done by people of lower rank. The basin and the towel are symbols of humble service. How can you wash the feet of someone today?

5. Walsh and Keesmaat, *Colossians Remixed*, 174.

6. Janet Boldt. Personal Conversation, August 26, 2014.

"Gentleness"

The perfect shirt to go with the pants of humility is gentleness. Empires and nations throughout history have established themselves and expanded through harsh aggression and violence, but the church is to wear the clothes of meekness, as some translations render it. The meek seek to be in dialogue with rather than overpowering the adversary. Gentleness is like the sun winning the contest over the wind where they compete to see who can remove a man's coat the fastest: the wind uses gale force in attempt to blow the coat off the man's back, only causing him to cling to it with greater tenacity, while the sun simply smiles with gentle warmth, and not long afterwards the man removes his coat with pleasure. The mature Christian is armed with the weapon that disarms: gentleness.

Smile and greet people warmly as persons made in the image of God.

"Patience"

A good illustration of the clothing of patience is to stalwartly wear the uniform of the Toronto Maple Leafs or the Vancouver Canucks! Both franchises have waited a long time to win the coveted Stanley Cup. We live in a society that demands instant gratification: fast food, drive through banking, high speed internet, instant messaging, "You can have it all now but you don't have to pay till next year!" A long building process is also not acceptable for a hockey team. Patience is about slowing down; about not having to get there immediately. The King James Version offers a wonderful synonym of patience: longsuffering. Perhaps some of our brothers and sisters in more hostile countries than ours have something to teach us about this item of clothing. Christians are people who wait: we wait for the reconciliation of all things as Christ has promised. Patience means that we do not take matters into our own hands but wait patiently for God to act, and then participate in what God is doing.

There are many places we are forced to wait during a typical day: at a traffic light, in a supermarket or bank line-up, at a doctor's office, for a young child to finish their vegetables. Take these moments to wait with purposeful awareness and patience.

We have this wonderful series of fancy clothes that look so nice. Shoes, socks, pants, shirt and tie: what else do we need? Who would ever argue with compassion, kindness, humility, gentleness, and patience?

"Forgiveness"

Communal life is not always tranquil and romantic, and relationships can become frayed and tattered. This is why Paul mentions the word for forgiveness three times! Things will go wrong when we live with other people. There will be differences, conflicts, quarrels, and spats. Forgiveness is essential if we want to live in harmony with other people. We not only forgive but we bear with one another—we keep on forgiving for the same things! We forgive because we have been forgiven. Do we keep repeating the same sins over and over? We have for generations! Does Christ's forgiveness continue to extend to us? Of course! This motivates us to continue to forgive when we are wronged.

Think of a relationship in your life or in our world that needs mending. Wear a band-aid on your hand to remind you to pray for forgiveness and healing in this relationship.

"Love"

Love is not just one of the qualities; it is the quality that is put on over all the other clothes and gives completeness. Love is the core and essence of what God is like. As the hymn-writer exalts, "The love of God is greater far than tongue or pen can ever tell. It goes beyond the highest star and reaches to the lowest hell."[7] The world was created by love, endures by love and is redeemed by love. "It is such

7. Frederick M. Lehman. "The Love of God." Public Domain, 1917.

love, in the face of all of the violence, selfishness, and narcissism of our times, that establishes community and sustains it."[8] Love completes the wardrobe, but there is still more to put on!

Communion is sometimes called the "Love Feast." It is much more than a thimble of grape juice and a cracker. Just as Jesus and his disciples sat down for a meal, so also do churches sometimes make the communion ritual part of a larger fellowship meal. This can also be practiced personally by inviting people over for a meal, perhaps someone you have not seen for a while, or bringing a meal to someone who is lonely and eating it with them.

"Peace"

It is a subversive irony to say that peace rules! Not a king or constitution, council or creed, but peace rules the church! In contrast to the violence of so-called imperial Pax-Romana and the present Pax-Americana, where peace is established by military force, Paul subverts this idea of peace by referring to a peace achieved through a victim of the empire: the crucified Christ. Victory comes through the cross and the empty tomb. The work of reconciliation—to bring peace to a relationship—is hard work. It is much easier to hold a grudge or to look for ways to get revenge. To truly get even with someone, though, should mean that both parties win and are dignified and uplifted.

Make a tight fist as you think of a situation of violence in your life, in your community, or in the wider world. Relax your fingers as you pray for peace in that situation.

"Thankfulness"

It is ironic that when we have less we are often more thankful for what we do have. When will we have enough? In contrast to the constant craving for more of our consumer culture, the mature Christian is called to gratitude and contentment. In contrast to a culture of

8. Walsh and Keesmaat, *Colossians Remixed*, 175.

dissatisfaction perpetuated by advertising and media, we are called to rest and be satisfied with everything that Christ gives. In Christ, we have all we need. The appropriate response is thankfulness.

Make a list of all the things and people you are thankful for; or, every day for a month, think of one different thing that you are thankful for.

"Indwelling message"

God wants to communicate with us; to this purpose, the Bible contains a message from God. For Christian maturity this message must take residence in us and become part of us. The best translation of this phrase is "Let the word of Christ dwell among you." This implies the corporate nature of the indwelling message. I grew up thinking that personal devotions were the highest form of scriptural study, yet we learn the message of Christ primarily in the context of the faith community. Although this can happen while listening to a sermon in church, it happens best around the dinner table in our homes or during the week at a small group gathering. It is a mutual sharing of the word. The message of the Gospel dwells in each one of us as individuals and among us in the community of faith. Letting the message of Jesus dwell in us is a process that takes time. patience!

Meditation is the spiritual discipline that would correspond with this process. Meditation is methodical and repetitive, like a cow chewing the cud over and over. Read a short text of Scripture and meditate on it. *Lectio Divina* is an ancient practice of Scripture meditation. The method is simple: Read a short portion of Scripture. What word or phrase catches your attention? Read it again. What message is there in this phrase? Read it a third time. How is God calling you to respond to this word?

"Worship in song"

Perhaps singing songs is the most flamboyant of the Christian clothes. The text says, "Teach and admonish one another by singing Psalms, hymns, and spiritual songs." Sometimes much has been made about the difference between psalms, hymns, and spiritual songs to try and create boundaries regarding the kind of songs we should sing in church, but really they are all the same. The important thing is that all these songs are consistent with the word of Christ. How do you teach theology most effectively? Sing it! Unfortunately, we do not always do it "with all wisdom."

Worship helps us develop the virtues we have mentioned previously. By singing songs of Christ we proclaim that Christ—not the global market, not the prime minister, not oil companies, not military might, not the mall—is the lord of our lives. "Jesus is Lord!" was the theme song of the early church. It was a statement of allegiance to another kingdom that was undermining the power of the empire. That is why they killed Christians in the first few centuries. These are controversial clothes! Worship was, and is, a politically subversive activity.

Go to church and participate in the singing. Gathering for special times of worship helps us to imagine what God wants us to be like the rest of the week. Getting together for an hour on Sunday morning may sometimes seem like the traditional thing to do—something we have done for generations without giving it any thought—but it is a radical statement of allegiance to a kingdom other than that of this world. The point is not to get some sort of kick out of the songs or to learn something revolutionary in the sermon. The point of singing a song of Christ, or wearing any one of the other items of communal clothing, is that it reminds us that it is not all about ourselves. It is about Christ being seen in us as a community; in how we live together with others. *Micah 6:8*

A Full Closet of Christian Maturity

The wardrobe of Christian maturity is filled with clothing that is completely out of style with the prevailing culture of consumerism, individualism, nationalism, militarism, and hedonism that attempts to sell itself as the latest and best when in actuality it is the tired, worn-out fashion that has been around for centuries. This is the clothing we are urged to strip off. The message of the Gospel in Colossians 3:12–17 offers us a different way to dress. We are invited to put on the precious hand-me-downs from God in Christ: compassion, kindness, humility, gentleness, patience, forgiveness, love, peace, thankfulness, an indwelling message, and worship in song.

Our journey of getting dressed began with the naked self and it ends in a communal dressing room. Human beings are created for relationship. Part of maturity is to become independent: to be able to dress yourself, feed yourself, and to look after yourself in various ways. Spiritual maturity also means that we begin to realize that we cannot make it on our own: we need other people in order to grow. Although the qualities of Christian maturity are inward qualities they are expressed in relationships with other people.

Throughout our lives we put on the clothes of gender, personality, age, family, history, culture, and painful experiences. All the things we have examined influence and shape us in profound ways. As followers of Christ we also desire to put on the clothes of our Leader. Jesus modelled this outfit for us in the few years he walked the dusty paths of Palestine. Now, it is our time to get dressed. We do not begin by shedding all the clothing that makes us who we are, but by examining each item carefully in light of this final wardrobe that Jesus modelled for us. Each one of us will wear it in our own unique way.

For Reflection

How would you define Christian maturity?

Which of the qualities from Colossians 3:12–17 appeal to you most? Why? Which ones seem like a difficult challenge? Why?

How will you put together the clothing of your life with the wardrobe of Christ?

Appendix 1

Enneagram Discernment Tool

How strongly do you identify with the following lists of words for each type? Rate each word on a scale of 1 (This does not describe me at all) to 5 (This describes me exactly) by circling the appropriate number.

The Heart Space:

#2 "The Helper"

- Caring   1 2 3 4 5
- People-oriented 1 2 3 4 5
- Generous   1 2 3 4 5
- Adaptable   1 2 3 4 5
- Sensitive   1 2 3 4 5

#3 "The Achiever"

- Motivated   1 2 3 4 5
- Competitive   1 2 3 4 5
- Ambitious   1 2 3 4 5
- Energetic   1 2 3 4 5
- Effective   1 2 3 4 5

#4 "The Individualist"

- Romantic   1 2 3 4 5
- Expressive   1 2 3 4 5
- Intense   1 2 3 4 5
- Unique   1 2 3 4 5
- Creative   1 2 3 4 5

The Head Space:

#5 "The Thinker"

- Observant   1 2 3 4 5
- Perceptive   1 2 3 4 5
- Analytical   1 2 3 4 5
- Logical   1 2 3 4 5
- Knowledgeable 1 2 3 4 5

#6 "The Loyalist"

- Questioning   1 2 3 4 5
- Faithful   1 2 3 4 5
- Cautious   1 2 3 4 5
- Supportive   1 2 3 4 5
- Discerning   1 2 3 4 5

#7 "The Enthusiast"

- Adventurous   1 2 3 4 5
- Spontaneous   1 2 3 4 5
- Happy   1 2 3 4 5
- Fun-loving   1 2 3 4 5
- Optimistic   1 2 3 4 5

The Gut Space:

#8 "The Leader"

- Courageous   1 2 3 4 5
- Self-confident   1 2 3 4 5
- Capable   1 2 3 4 5
- Assertive   1 2 3 4 5
- Direct   1 2 3 4 5

#9 "The Peacemaker"

- Pleasant   1 2 3 4 5
- Patient   1 2 3 4 5
- Open-minded   1 2 3 4 5
- Harmonious   1 2 3 4 5
- Easy-going   1 2 3 4 5

#1 "The Reformer"

- Perfectionist   1   2   3   4   5
- Reliable   1   2   3   4   5
- Hard-working   1   2   3   4   5
- Organized   1   2   3   4   5
- Principled   1   2   3   4   5

Now add up the totals for each type. Those with the highest totals will indicate your predominant spiritual types. Consider also which of the three centres you found yourself in to help you differentiate between a few that may have high totals. Completing other tests, reading a book, and spending time in prayer and reflection will also be helpful.

Appendix 2

Family Systems Discernment Tool[1]

THIS TOOL IS NOT a measurement of the health or dysfunction of your family. It is merely a way to assist in identifying the primary system of our family of origin.

Adaptability Scale:

The adaptability scale ranges from chaotic to rigid. Most families will tend toward one or the other. To help discern your family's system rate each statement on a scale of 1 (almost always true for my family) to 5 (almost never true for my family).

- We spent a lot of time talking but rarely came to a decision.

  1 2 3 4 5

- Children basically did their own thing.

  1 2 3 4 5

- Rules changed with the circumstances.

  1 2 3 4 5

- All types of feelings were freely expressed.

  1 2 3 4 5

- Plans were held loosely and were easily changed.

  1 2 3 4 5

1. Based on Stoop, *Forgiving Our Parents*, 76–90.

Add up the total. A number below 15 would indicate a tendency toward being a chaotic family. A number above 15 would indicate a tendency toward being a rigid family.

Attachment Scale:

The attachment scale ranges from disengaged to enmeshed. Most families will tend toward one or the other. To help discern your family's system rate each statement on a scale of 1 (almost always true for my family) to 5 (almost never true for my family).

- We shared deep feelings with each other.

    1 2 3 4 5

- When there was a problem we would stick together.

    1 2 3 4 5

- We did a lot of things together.

    1 2 3 4 5

- My family members were my best friends.

    1 2 3 4 5

- Family gatherings were very important.

    1 2 3 4 5

Add up the total. A number below 15 would indicate a tendency toward being an enmeshed family. A number above 15 would indicate a tendency toward being a disengaged family.

Appendix 3

A Letter from Nelleken Jasper

WARM GREETINGS TO YOU all, my dear sisters and brothers in the Lord. My friends, you need to know that I am happy and doing well. My mind has not changed and I will continue to stick to the eternal truth till my dying breath.

Let me tell you what happened to me. I was brought before the leaders. There were four of them: the governor, two judges and the clerk of the court. When I came into the room I bowed to them and the governor said, "Greetings, my daughter, how are you?" I replied, "Quite well sir." He asked me if I was not tired of sitting in jail here and I said, "Yes, I am, why don't you do away with me sooner rather than later. You've killed my parents and my two friends and I miss them very much." The governor said, "Don't talk like this my child. Give up your stubborn opinions and you can go free. It would make me too sad to do this to you. You haven't been baptized; you have no reason to be here. Give it up!"

The judge asked the governor, "She has not yet been baptized?" "No," I said, "I have not been baptized, but if you released me tonight, I would be baptized by tomorrow, I promise you!" Then they sighed over me and I said, "The two boys were not baptized either." They replied, "That is true, we tried to change their opinions but they would not budge." And I said, "I won't leave my faith commitment either!" They warned me that I could suffer the same fate and I said, "Go ahead, roast me on a rotisserie, boil me in oil, I will continue to trust that God's grace will keep me in his truth till my dying breath. You might as well do it today rather than wait till tomorrow."

I firmly hope and trust in God that he will help me. I have fixed my confidence in the word, where it says, "Oh my chosen, do not be afraid; I will protect you in fire and in water, and I will not allow you to be tempted above what you are able to bear."

Then they said, "Daughter, you've been deceived, your parents led you astray, you were only a child; they had authority over you and you in your innocence followed them. Now you have grown up a little and are out from under their influence. Surely you have the ability to make up your own mind. Give up your silly opinions and the king will pardon you. You are young yet. You are beautiful. You could get married to a fine young man."

I said that I surely do have my own mind and that I would rather keep what I have in the present. They said I should take some time to think about it and I said that I had thought about it enough already and wasn't about to change for their sake.

They tried another approach. "What about your soul? Don't you want to be saved and go to heaven?" I told them that many people just want an easy ticket to heaven but that few were willing to suffer with Christ. They argued that being a Christian had little to do with suffering. I said, "Christ himself had to suffer, how much more do we?" but they did not reply to this and instead said that I could talk to some priests about it. I said I wasn't at all interested in this; that I wanted to keep what I had. They said, "If you died tonight you would go straight to hell. Your parents and your two friends would be glad to be in your place, to have another chance to change their minds." I said that I knew better than that!

We talked and argued a lot more but it would take me too long to write it all, and besides, I've forgotten much of it. So my dear friends, whom I love from my deepest heart, please pray for me that I will be able to end my life to the praise of God.

Dear friends, I have to be honest with you, I still may have to go through a great desert and sometimes I am very scared. This is a lonely and dangerous place. It's like walking through thistles and thorns. But I also know that a crown of life is prepared for us. We have the right truth and I don't think any other will ever be found. God is a faithful supporter, a strength in weakness, and a comforter in sad times. Let us snuggle close in God's arms and throw all our anxieties on God for God cares for us and will watch over us. One day we will all be together, sitting around the table in heaven.

And so I commend you to the Lord, to the mighty word of grace. May the peace of God rule in your hearts. Say hi to all my friends.

Sincerely,

Nelleken Jasper, a girl from Blijenburg,
your unworthy sister in the Lord,

December 12, 1569.

P.S. Please write back. I would love to get a letter sometime.[2]

2. This version of the letter is edited and paraphrased by the author using Augsburger, *Faithful Unto Death*, and Van Braght, *Martyr's Mirror*.

Bibliography

à Kempis, Thomas. Edited by Harold C. Gardiner. *The Imitation of Christ*. New York: Doubleday, 1955.

Altson, Renée. *Stumbling Toward Faith*. El Cajon, CA: Youth Specialties, 2004.

Arnett, Jeffrey Jensen. *Adolescence and Emerging Adulthood*. Upper Saddle River, NJ: Prentice-Hall, 2004.

Augsburger, David. *Dissident Discipleship: A Spirituality of Self-Surrender, Love of God, and Love of Neighbor*. Grand Rapids: Brazos, 2006.

Augsburger, Myron. *Faithful Unto Death*. Waco, TX: Word, 1978.

Balswick, Jack O., Pamela Ebstyne King, and Kevin S. Reimer. *The Reciprocating Self: Human Development in Theological Perspective*. Downers Grove, IL: InterVarsity, 2005.

Baron, Renee, and Elizabeth Wagele. *The Enneagram Made Easy*. San Francisco: HarperCollins, 1994.

Beaudoin, Tom. *Consuming Faith: Integrating Who We Are with What We Buy*. Landham, MD: Sheed & Ward, 2003.

———. *Virtual Faith: The Irreverent Quest of Generation X*. San Francisco: Jossey-Bass, 1998.

Bell, Rob. *SexGod: Exploring the Endless Connection between Sexuality and Spirituality*. Grand Rapids: Zondervan, 2007.

Bergin, Eilis, and Eddie Fitzgerald. *An Enneagram Guide: A Spirituality of Love in Brokenness*. Mystic, CT: Twenty-Third, 1993.

Bibby, Reginald W. *The Emerging Millennials*. Toronto: Project Canada, 2009.

Bly, Robert. *Iron John*. Boston: Addison-Wesley, 1990.

Boriase, Craig. *The Naked Christian: Taking Off Religion to Find True Relationship*. Winter Park, FL: Relevant, 2005.

Bowler, Kate. *Blessed: A History of the American Prosperity Gospel*. New York: Oxford University Press, 2013.

Brandt, Gareth. "Transformation: Becoming Who God Created Us to Be." *The Messenger*, July 5, 2006, 4–6.

———. *Under Construction: Reframing Men's Spirituality*. Waterloo, ON: Herald, 2009.

———. *Young Adult Spirituality: The Transition from Adolescence to Maturity*. Saskatoon Theological Union: STM thesis, 1997.

Brueggemann, Walter. *The Bible Makes Sense*. Winona, MN: St. Mary's, 1977.

Burke, Spencer, and Barry Taylor. *A Heretic's Guide to Eternity*. San Francisco: Jossey-Bass, 2006.

Cairns, Earle E. *An Endless Line of Splendor: Revivals and their Leaders from the Great Awakening to the Present*. Wheaton, IL: Tyndale, 1986.

Cavanaugh, William T. *Being Consumed: Economics and Christian Desire*. Grand Rapids: Eerdmans, 2008.

The Confessions of St. Augustine. Translated by John K. Ryan. New York: Doubleday, 1960.

Conn, Joann Wolski. *Women's Spirituality: Resources for Christian Development*. New York: Paulist, 1986.

Cruz, Nicky. *Run Baby Run*. Gainsville, FL: Bridge-Logos, 1968.

Dark, David. *The Sacredness of Questioning Everything*. Grand Rapids: Zondervan, 2009.

Dean, Kenda Creasy. "Holding On to Our Kisses: The Hormonal Theology of Adolescence." *1999 Princeton Lectures on Youth, Church, and Culture*, Princeton Theological Seminary, 2000.

———. "How to Avoid Raising Nice Teenagers." *Christian Research Journal* 34:5 (2011), 36–38.

———. "X-Files and Unknown Gods: The Search for Truth with Postmodern Adolescents" *American Baptist Quarterly* 49.1 (March 2000), 3–21.

Edwards, Jonathan. Edited by John Smith. *Concerning the Religious Affections*. New Haven: Yale University Press, 1959.

Erikson, Millard J. *Postmodernizing the Faith*. Grand Rapids: Baker, 1998.

Fellman, Walter, editor. *Selected Writings of Hans Denck*. Pittsburgh: Pickwick, 1975.

Ford, Iris. *Life Spirals*. Toronto: Welch, 1988.

Foster, Richard J. *Streams of Living Water: Celebrating the Great Traditions of Christian Faith*. San Francisco: HarperCollins, 1998.

Fowler, James. *Becoming Adult, Becoming Christian*. San Francisco: Jossey-Bass, 2001.

———. *Stages of Faith: The Psychology of Human Development and the Quest for Meaning*. San Francisco: HarperCollins, 1981.

Gillis, John R. *Youth and History*. San Diego: Academic, 1981.

Hagberg, Janet O., and Robert A. Guelich. *The Critical Journey: Stages in the Life of Faith*. Salem, WI: Sheffield, 2005.

Harder, Leland, editor. *The Sources of Swiss Anabaptism*. Kitchener, ON: Herald, 1985.

Henson, John. *Good as New: A Radical Retelling of the Scriptures*. Winchester, UK: John Hunt, 2004.

Hess, Carol Lakey. *Caretakers of Our Common House: Women's Development in Communities of Faith*. Nashville: Abingdon, 1997.

Hughes, Gerard. *God of Surprises*. London, UK: Darton, Longman & Todd, 2008.

Jethani, Skye. *The Divine Commodity*. Grand Rapids: Zondervan, 2009.

Jones, Stephen. *Faith Shaping*. Valley Forge, PA: Judson, 1987.

BIBLIOGRAPHY

Jones, Tony. *Postmodern Youth Ministry*. El Cajon, CA: Youth Specialties, 2001.

Levinson, Daniel J. *The Seasons of a Man's Life*. New York: Ballantine, 1978.

Keating, Charles J. *Who We Are is How We Pray*. Mystic, CT: Twenty-Third, 1987.

Kraus, C. Norman. *Using Scripture in a Global Age*. Telford, PA: Cascadia, 2006.

McLaren, Brian. *Naked Spirituality*. San Francisco: Jossey-Bass, 2011

———. *A New Kind of Christian*. SanFrancisco: Jossey-Bass, 2001.

Miller, Donald. *Blue Like Jazz: Nonreligious Thoughts on Christian Spirituality*. Nashville: Thomas Nelson, 2003.

———. *Father Fiction: Chapters for a Fatherless Generation*. New York: Howard, 2010.

Murray, Stuart. *The Naked Anabaptist: The Bare Essentials of a Radical Faith*. Waterloo, ON: Herald, 2010.

Myers, Isabel Briggs, with Peter B. Myers. *Gifts Differing: Understanding Personality Type*. Palo Alto, CA: Davies-Black, 1995.

Newell, J. Philip. *One Foot in Eden: A Celtic View of the Stages of Life*. New York: Paulist, 1999.

Norris, Kathleen. *Amazing Grace: A Vocabulary of Faith*. New York: Riverhead, 1998.

Nouwen, Henri. *Wounded Healer*. New York: Doubleday, 1979.

———. *Life of the Beloved: Spiritual Living in a Secular World*. New York: Crossroad, 2002.

Palmer, Parker. *Let your Life Speak*. San Francisco: Jossey-Bass, 2000.

Parks, Sharon Daloz. *Big Questions, Worthy Dreams*. San Francisco: Jossey-Bass, 2000.

———. *The Critical Years*. San Francisco: Harper & Row, 1986.

Peck, M. Scott. *The Road Less Travelled*. New York: Simon & Schuster, 1978.

Peterson, Eugene. *Answering God: The Psalms as Tools for Prayer*. San Francisco: HarperCollins, 1989.

Powers, Rosemary. *The Celtic Quest: Contemporary Celtic Spirituality*. Dublin, IRL: Columba, 2010.

Rambo, Lewis. *Understanding Religious Conversion*. New Haven, CT: Yale University Press, 1993.

Reese, Randy. *Deep Mentoring: Guiding Others on their Leadership Journey*. Downers Grove, IL: InterVarsity, 2012.

Roehlkepartain, Eugene C., and Donald L. Griggs. *The Teaching Church*. Nashville: Abingdon, 1993.

Rohr, Richard. *The Enneagram: A Christian Perspective*. New York: Crossroad, 2001.

———. *From Wild Man to Wise Man*. Cincinnati, OH: St. Anthony Messenger, 2005.

———. *Immortal Diamond: The Search for Our True Self*. San Francisco: Jossey-Bass, 2013.

———. *The Naked Now: Learning to See as the Mystics See*. New York: Crossroad, 2009.

Rollins, Peter. *How (Not) to Speak of God*. Brewster, MA: Paraclete, 2006.

Schaff, Philip, editor. *A Select Library of the Nicene and Post-Nicene Fathers of the Christian Church, Volume VII*. Grand Rapids: Eerdmans, 1956.

Schwarz, Christian A. *The 3 Colors of Your Spirituality*. St. Charles, IL: ChurchSmart, 2009.

Slee, Nicola. *Women's Faith Development: Patterns and Processes*. Aldershot, UK: Ashgate, 2004.

Smith, Christian, with Patricia Snell. *Souls in Transition: The Religious & Spiritual Lives of Emerging Adults*. New York: Oxford University Press, 2009.

Smith, Gordon. *Beginning Well: Christian Conversion and Authentic Transformation*. Downers Grove, IL: InterVarsity, 2001.

————. *Called to Be Saints: An Invitation to Christian Maturity*. Downers Grove, IL: IVP Academic, 2014.

Snyder, C. Arnold. *Following in the Footsteps of Christ: The Anabaptist Tradition*. Maryknoll, NY: Orbis, 2004.

Stoop, David. *Forgiving our Parents Forgiving our Selves*. Ann Arbour, MI: Servant, 1991.

Thomas, Gary L. *Sacred Pathways: Discover Your Soul's Path to God*. Grand Rapids: Zondervan, 2000.

Thompson, Marjorie J. *Family the Forming Center*. Nashville: Upper Room, 1996.

Tomkins, Stephen, and Dan Graves, editors. *The Four Loves by St Bernard of Clairvaux. From Public Domain material at Christian Classics Ethereal Library at Calvin College*. No pages. Online: http://www.ccel.org/ccel/bernard/loving_god.pdf

Van Braght, Thieleman. *Martyrs Mirror*. Scottdale, PA: Herald, 1950.

Walsh, Brian, and Sylvia Keesmaat. *Colossians Remixed*. Downers Grove, IL: InterVarsity, 2004.

Walsh, Brian. *Truth is Stranger than it Used to Be: Biblical Faith in a Postmodern Age*. Downers Grove, IL: IVP Academic, 1995.

Weisberger, Bernard A. *They Gathered at the River: The Story of the Great Revivalists and their Impact upon Religion in America*. New York: Quadrangle, 1958.

Wuthnow, Robert. *After the Baby Boomers: How Twenty- and Thirty-Somethings Are Shaping the Future of American Religion*. Princeton, NJ: Princeton University Press, 2007.

York, Tripp. *The Purple Crown: The Politics of Martyrdom*. Waterloo, ON: Herald, 2007.

Zuercher, Suzanne. *Enneagram Spirituality: From Compulsion to Contemplation*. Notre Dame, IN: Ave Maria, 1992.